THE FREE CITY

BY

WILLIS NUTTING

TEMPLEGATE PUBLISHERS

SPRINGFIELD, ILLINOIS

1

Public discussion has a way of concerning itself with secondary questions before it has found an answer to primary ones, and therefore the heat generated in argument produces much emotion and consequent propaganda, but very little light. This is certainly true of our discussion of higher education. We get enthusiastic; we think that the welfare of our country demands more than we have now; and we lose our tempers over whether governmental aid should go to private as well as to public institutions. But we have not seriously concerned ourselves with the problem of what higher education is, what it should accomplish, and what money has to do with it.

We would probably, most of us, grant that the arts of the beauty parlor and the undertaker would not be included in higher education, and that the art of expressing one's self in English would be included, but that is about the limit of our precision. Just why we would exclude embalming and include basket weaving is not clear, or why we should include basket weaving and leave out theology.

We are sure that higher education is to accomplish something very good, but when we try to determine just what that something is we are by no means so sure. Even in the pronouncements of our educational leaders there is confusion. If sufficient money is given to higher education, they seem to say, our colleges and universities will produce highly trained experts—scientists, engineers and scholars—who will push forward the frontiers of knowledge in their own special directions and will help the country get ahead of the Russians. Besides this they seem to be telling us that these same schools by giving this same education to these same people will be developing intellects to the fullest capacity. And

3

then they seem to assume that men so trained and with intellects so developed will almost automatically become better leaders of society and will thus enable democracy to function better. There is little discussion of *how* or *whether* the training necessary to produce the expert develops the mind to its fullest capacity, or of how or whether such education makes men better civic leaders. So the schools go on their confused and confusing way, asking for money to enable them to train the needed specialists who as a matter of course will be wise men and will lead us to a better world.

This whole question of the fundamental aims and practices of higher education needs very much to be taken apart and looked at more closely than has been the case up to now. In the first place, there is definitely a before and after in the educational process. A man is a person before he is a civic leader or an expert. Therefore it would seem sensible to give priority of concern in higher education to the man himself, so that if possible he may become wise and understanding. This is true even if the ultimate aim is to make him an expert or a leader.

In the second place, it is by no means certain that the kind of training necessary to make a man a specialist will also fully develop his intellect. It is even likely that such training so narrows his interests and his ability to think in many directions that he becomes less wise than he was before he began his training.

In the third place it is quite possible (and this possibility seems to by supported by considerable empirical evidence) that the almost exclusively theoretical education that a person gets in college positively *unfits* him for leading men. He is "educated away" from his fellows so that he can no longer communicate with them.

Thus it is possible that in the confusion of aims proclaimed by college spokesmen one aim cancels out the others, so that nothing happens in regard to the golden hope of education that has been held out to us.

Lord Acton speaks of an English Prime Minister who for the first half of his term was head of the most radical government in Europe. His government in the last half of the term was the most conservative, and the man himself never knew the difference. And the world has seen some very eminent physicists and engineers who have seemed willing to serve the Nazis, the Communists, or the government of the United States with equal eagerness, depending on who had possession of them at the moment and would provide them with working facilities. The world has also seen theologians who have flown the flag of whatever party was in power regardless of what the party stood for. There was nothing in their fields of expertness that would tell these men the difference. But as *men* they should have known. Because they were in positions of influence they should have had an education beyond their specialties, an education that would point them toward wisdom, so as to have known whom they could rightly support or cooperate with.

The expert and the potential civic leader need education as men—and this is called liberal education—before they start to fulfill their special functions; and liberal education must be that which helps them become wise and understanding. Only then will it be safe for society to allow them to exercise the very dangerous influence that expertness and the ability to lead gives them.

Our liberal arts colleges in our universities and our private colleges claim to give this necessary liberal education. But here again there is a need for examination. Nowhere in higher education is there so much confusion of aims and practices as we find among the advocates of liberal education. There is indecision as to the goals, and almost no investigation as to whether the academic practices in vogue in our liberal colleges actually lead to any goal at all.

These liberal colleges are almost all of them using or trying to use the methods and ideals developed in the nineteenth century for the training of expert scholars. We find them employing as teachers men who are or hope to be expert scholars themselves, men whose recognized success depends more on their scholarship, their "competence in their field," than on their teaching.

At the worst these men are only interested in working at their specialty, and regard teaching as an unfortunate necessity forced upon them by their need of a livelihood. This is of course recognized as bad, but what is considered good might be in reality even worse for the students. One of these scholars might also be a

5

brilliant teacher, able to inspire multitudes of young people. Then what happens? The teacher inspires them with a love and enthusiasm for his own subject, and the love and enthusiasm so inspired has as a side effect the students' growing lack of interest in other subjects, which then usually leads to a positive contempt of them. Thus the student is led by the good teacher into a disastrous narrow-mindedness. Our liberal colleges are full of good scholar-teachers who proceed solemnly through the years building up devoted followings of young people blind to the splendor of all the truth save one little particle.

Under these conditions the liberal college becomes a battle ground where specialist scholars compete with one another for the time, the interest, and the very souls of their students, and where these same scholars jostle each other to get courses of their departments on the "required" list and to get courses of other departments removed from it. Each teacher piles the work on the students, knowing that his teacher-competitor is also piling it on, and that unless he loads the student with enough work the student will be compelled to devote less time to his course than to the courses of the teachers who require more.

The mind of the student is pulled seven ways in this turmoil. He is almost forced to give his allegiance somewhere, and this means "disallegiance" elsewhere. How a harmonious and well-balanced development of the intellect—either the intellect of the student or of the teacher—can be hoped for in such a situation is not easily seen. Yet almost the only students who avoid becoming partisans are the ones whose interest is aroused nowhere.

The good science major has, almost as a part of his excellence, a contempt for philosophy, literature and history. The good history major has a contempt for science, literature and philosophy. The good literature man has a contempt for the precision of scientific knowledge—and so on. It seems that special interest in one field of knowledge carries with it a loyalty which expresses itself in an antagonistic attitude toward all other knowledge. This is not wisdom. It is narrowness. It is the expression of a mis-educated intellect, and an indication of the mis-education of the scholar-teachers who seem to delight in communicating this at-

6

titude to their students. Yet this is what successful liberal education in our colleges results in. Unsuccessful liberal education results in the student's lack of interest in anything intellectual.

The unfortunate narrowness of good students comes, I think, from the wrong ideal that colleges have cherished and have tried to impart to their students: *the specialist scholar as the paradigm, the highest and best example, of the man whose intellect is fully and rightly developed.* Each college hopes that it can produce more than its share of scholars. Each college consoles itself with the possibility that its less brilliant students, who will not become brilliant scholars, can at least become mediocre (and so even the more stupid students are required to write "research" papers with footnotes). Every college prides itself on the number of its students who go on to graduate schools and on the number of distinguished scholars it can attract to its faculty to serve as dazzling examples to the students and as occasions of envy on the part of rival colleges.

Here, now, is the central question: *Is* the specialist scholar the paradigm of the "imperial intellect," the best example of the well developed mind? Does he as a matter of fact have that well balanced intellect that a liberal education is supposed to give? I would answer definitely, "No." The scholar as such tends to be narrow, and blind in spots. He is not outstandingly wise or understanding. He is factional, contentious, and eager to win an argument rather than to know.

But if the scholar as such does not happen to be the intellectual hero our academic ideal supposes him to be, then the whole orientation of our liberal colleges is wrong from start to finish. Their practices, their theories and their personnel—all these are set up to prevent the accomplishment of what these colleges claim to intend to accomplish: the leading of young people to wisdom and understanding through a harmonious development of the mind.

There is no doubt that to train specialist scholars you need specialist scholars as teachers. But to educate liberally you need teachers who are seeking in themselves the wisdom and understanding, the breadth of interest and the respect for all knowledge, that the school wishes to impart to its students. This is not what the specialist scholar seeks primarily. And to educate liberally you need methods which are calculated to lead students to wisdom and understanding rather than to "learning," for wisdom and understanding do not necessarily come as an end-product of the process of accumulating learning. (By learning *here* we mean what a "learned man" possesses.)

If there is to be a genuine liberal education there must be a breaking of the traditional academic bonds that have confined teaching and learning to the narrow methods and ideals sanctioned and required by the professional scholars (and by learning *here* we mean the general acquiring of *knowledge*). There must be among those who control and practice liberal education an ability to imagine an educational atmosphere and pattern quite different from anything among us now. Einstein has said that an untrammeled imagination is necessary for any advance of knowledge anywhere. Let us see where such imagining might take us as we try to construct a plan of liberal education which would really educate people liberally.

As a preliminary we must make a deeper investigation of the situation of the specialist scholar and his influence on the popular idea of the liberal college.

* * *

2

I am Benjamin Jowett

Master of Balliol College.

What is worth knowing, I know it.

What I don't know is not knowledge.

Thus the Oxford students of an earlier day poked fun at one of their luminaries, and their little rhyme could very well fit the attitude of our present intellectual leaders. But with one correction: our scholars do not say, "What is worth knowing *I* know it," but each group of scholarly specialists acts as though it were saying, "What is worth knowing *we* know it, and what we don't know, or can't know by our method of finding out truth, is not knowledge."

There is a profound and genuine humility among our scholars, but it is a most narrow humility, functioning well before truth which can be gained by a certain accepted method and before scholars who use that method well. But there is a terrifying collective arrogance toward truth that is claimed by seekers who follow other methods. Anything outside one's own general field of interest is "not knowledge," or "meaningless," or "lyric"— something to which the category of true-or-false cannot be applied. This is too often the characteristic attitude of the academic man.

The humility of the scientist, for instance, has become proverbial, and it is quite true that he is humble before evidence collected by a scientific method and before conclusions inferred from such evidence. But he is likely to be supremely arrogant toward evidence and conclusions accepted by, say, theologians, or

9

toward the value judgments of the moralist, or toward the insights reached by the *esprit de finesse* of the literary man. The scientist is just as arrogant as were the earlier theologians toward his scientific predecessors, and just as obscurantist.

The narrowness of the scientist is especially evident now because he dominates the intellectual field, but it is not the only narrowness. The same narrow outlook was present in the philosophers of the sixteenth and seventeenth centuries in their insistence upon arguing from philosophical principles to the facts of nature and in their refusal to recognize the value of the experimental-mathematical method of the founders of the new natural science. We can detect it in the contemporary historians who think that to account for the historical origins of an idea is to say all that can be said of its meaning and validity. I have heard a distinguished professor of History maintain in a public lecture that the value of Socrates's argument for submitting to the law that condemned him was entirely dependent on his actual authorship of the argument. The validity of the Socratic teaching stands or falls with the historicity of Socrates! And we find it in the frightening blindness of the English Major in college, who will not see any difference between what is factual and what is imaginative, between what is historical and what is fictional, who thinks that the mind, because it has a creative function, does not also have a function in which it is formed by something other than itself, and who makes a cult of imprecision and inexactness.

It seems that each intellectual holds tight to the truth that is reached by a method that he accepts. He nurses it, meditates on it, perhaps extends it, and evaluates everything in terms of it. He cannot understand, and therefore is inclined to dismiss, purported knowledge reached in other ways.

This situation is not hard to understand psychologically. Each method of getting at the truth requires the use of certain capacities of the mind. To think out a theorem of geometry, for instance, is a thinking different from that required for figuring out whether or not Mary Queen of Scots murdered her husband.

When a person follows for some time a certain way of thinking in order to discover a certain kind of truth, he can become expert in that way, quick to see implications and irrelevances,

10

skillful at coming to conclusions. The more he applies himself to his way the greater is the facility gained and the results obtained. He can become an authority, before whom beginners in that way of knowing stand in awe. His very success can (and often does) so dazzle him and his admirers that they assume that the particular light they see is the only light there is.

Here is the narrowness: that same concentration which enables the thinker to get so far in his particular kind of knowing, that same enthusiasm which leads him on in his investigation of that particular truth, helps him to become less facile and less interested in other ways of thinking; and finally the reality and even the possibility of anything of value coming out of other ways escapes him entirely. The old definition of the specialist as one who comes to know more and more about less and less describes rather accurately the potential narrowness which threatens the full intellectual development of the "intellectual."

Thus the truth lies in pieces, and the defenders of each piece deny the value and perhaps the very reality of the other pieces. And there are pieces within pieces. Perhaps the most fundamental split separating the discoverers and communicators of truth is the split between those who in their operation use words with one precise meaning and those who use words—perhaps the same words—which trail clouds of connotation. The sentences of the latter, the poets, can seem quite meaningless to the former, the scientists and historians. These users of precise words do not necessarily reject poetry altogether. They may respect its esthetic value. But they find it hard to think of it as a way of knowing reality and of communicating that knowledge.

There is also a split in the ranks of the non-poets which is almost as deep and which may be even more significant in the splintering truth. This is the separation between the mathematicians and natural scientists on the one side, and on the other the followers of the *Philosophia Perennis*—the metaphysical and ethical thinking that has come down from the Greeks as a part of the Western tradition.

The distinction, so popular now, that places our educated people in two cultural worlds, the world of science and the world of the humanities, is thus inaccurate. The situation is more compli-

11

cated. Historical thinking, for instance, is almost as different from physics as it is from poetry, and the cultural world of the *Philosophia Perennis* is just as alien to the humanist as it is to the chemist. This latter cultural world is not now inhabited by too many people, but it once was dominant with us, so that if we are unfamiliar with it we are cut off from our own ancestors. Moreover, such a lack of understanding puts us completely out of touch with the kind of thinking that gave rise to the basic ideas by which we live—the idea of justice and its importance, the idea of human equality, the idea of the rights of man, and the idea of a political society. If this realm of thinking comes to be completely neglected, it could well be that these ideas will cease to be valued.

Besides these great gaps yawning between the separate groups of thinking men, which constitute real dangers to the unity of our society, there are smaller gaps of mutual intolerance and lack of understanding. Get a physicist, for example, to tell you what he really thinks of the science of sociology.

This all adds up to the fact that our specialist scholars, the men who teach in our colleges and who set the tone for the intellectual side of our culture, are narrow and one-sided, not wise and therefore not truly intellectual in the sense of having full intellectual development. For when a man holds on to only a splinter of truth he is not wise, however learned he may be. The wise man understands and sympathizes with all seekers after truth. He respects them and tries to understand the methods by which they work, the criteria by which they judge their results, and the kind of certainty they have a right to claim. This does not mean of course that he must agree with everything they say, but it does mean that when he disagrees it is with full understanding of what he disagrees with. And the wise man must keep an "open end" in his thinking. He must never say, "This is all the truth there is," or—here is where very many learned men are not wise—"These are the only methods by which truth can be reached." He must never allow himself in any way to be implicated in that supreme attitude of unwisdom: What I don't know is not knowledge. He must never block the way of inquiry.

It is because of the splintering of truth that the great increase in knowledge in the last few centuries has not led to an increase of wisdom. It would be hazardous to claim, in the light of their sayings and of their actions, that the men who are the custodians of this new knowledge have any more wisdom than those totally innocent of book-learning.

The splintering can be explained philosophically and also historically: philosophically by the fact that the intellectual world has adopted Descartes' error of assuming that all truth can be gained by the use of one method and one set of criteria and that whatever cannot be attained by this method and validated by these criteria must be rejected as false; and historically, by the decline of the great intellectual dialogue in which the Western intellectual tradition was established.

But just now we must notice one very great danger that comes from this breaking-up of the block of total truth: the fact that it is to these narrow specialists of knowledge that we entrust the education of young people who are awakening to the joy of using their intellects, who are becoming capable of glimpsing the splendor of truth. With such tutors what likelihood is there that young people, coming into the age of realization, will be able to appreciate the whole of that splendor, or even know that there is a whole? The ones who teach them do not see it. The textbooks they study do not show it. Where will they learn about it? And how then, when young people are thus educated, will they become wise and understanding?

It is obvious that we live in the age of the expert. Anyone who wants to be anything must possess some special skill at doing some one thing. But as people and society come more and more into the hands of experts, it becomes more and more necessary that what the experts do be guided by wisdom; and wisdom does not lie within the realm of any kind of expertness. The expert—and this includes the scholarly specialist as well as the technician—must either have the wisdom to use his expertness well and rightly, to know when, where and even whether to use the skill that he possesses; or else he becomes merely an instrument, powerful but blind, to function at the command of someone else, whether that someone be a government, a corporation, or the president of a university. The specialist without wisdom, then, can be a sinister being, an effective utensil in the hands of someone other than himself. He has abdicated the responsibility of deciding the occasions of exercising his own skill. The rocket expert willing to work for any government or any corporation that will finance his operations and giving no thought to his responsibility for what is done with the rockets he produces, is such a sinister instrument. We are aware that responsibility ought to go with political power; but that responsibility ought to go with knowledge also, and that therefore a learned person has an obligation to seek after wisdom, seems to have escaped many scholars.

In these days when it is more true than ever that knowledge is power, it is more true than ever that those who know must assume the obligation of seeing that their knowledge is put to *good* use. The specialist scholar as such is narrow. He is almost compelled by the requirements of his profession to be narrow unless he is man enough to transcend them.

But the whole scholarly community, as it has grown up in our Western world, is also narrow. It specializes in theory—the relation of ideas to one another—and is almost wholly innocent of that other very real kind of knowing: the understanding of particular things, persons and situations. It is this lack of understanding of the particular that so often makes the scholar helpless in the hands of the practical man, and so easily manipulated. This kind of narrowness in the scholarly world, a narrowness that makes its members so often incapable of decision in existential situations, can never be removed by the program of the many sincere reformers who wish to improve our system of higher education by making it more like that of Western Europe. European scholars are as helpless as our own in the face of existential reality. Witness how often they have wilted in the face of totalitarian brutality.

Narrowness, then, is a characteristic of our intellectuals. They do not understand each other and they do not understand the actual situations of life. Insofar as they are narrow they have been mis-educated. That this mis-education can be remedied is the thesis of this book, but before we can proceed to consider it we must point out that so long as this particular "narrowness-producing" education continues, just so long will the Great American Hope in education continue to be frustrated: the hope that our educational system is producing wise leaders.

The dream of the philosopher-king has been with us for two millennia and more. Whoever has the job of ruling ought to have at his disposal the wisdom of the ages. The man who has spent his life developing his mind ought to make his community's vital decisions more wisely than the uneducated man. At the back of our minds, at least, we assume this to be true, and we take it for granted that our institutions of higher learning are in some measure preparing men to rule wisely.

In indulging this hope, in which we have been willing to invest billions, we have been deceiving ourselves. Our institutions of higher learning have not been educating men to be good leaders, for good leaders are men who make wise decisions. They are training men to be scholars. Scholars will at most be members of advisory boards and discussion panels, "resource men" whose advice is perhaps asked by the decision-makers and perhaps followed. Our philosophers are not kings. They do not make the decisions.

The men who actually make the decisions, who take the advice of the learned men or ignore it, are not the pride of our colleges. Most of them are men whose training has been acquired in practical politics, law or business. They know how to handle men and situations, but very few of them have at their disposal enough theoretical knowledge to enable them to decide wisely. We desperately need wisdom in the decisions our leaders make. We are lucky to get practical cleverness.

It is easy for our intellectuals to treat our practical men with contempt and to blame our people for not choosing scholars to govern them. It is easy for scholars to lament the anti-intellectualism of American life. But the answer to such a complaint is simple: Look at the intellectuals! Who would want to be led by one of them? The common man rightly distrusts the "egg-head," not because the egg-head knows so much, but because there is so much that he does not know. Our learned people and our practical people differ, not in that the former know and the latter do not know, but in that the former have one kind of knowledge (and ignorance) and the latter another.

This distinction between the two kinds of necessary knowledge is not the old Greek distinction between speculative and practical. We can leave practical knowledge out of consideration for the moment. The distinction lies within the realm of speculative knowledge itself, knowledge for its own sake. Within this field of knowledge sought for its own sake there are two kinds of things to be investigated and understood. On the one hand there is the determining of the meaning and relationship of *ideas,* an intellectual activity which results in science when its object is elaborated and made precise. On the other hand there is the understanding of *particular things*—individual events, situations and men *in their uniqueness.* Both kinds of knowing are necessary if a person is to understand the world and what goes on in it. But the intellectual has the first kind of knowledge and is almost entirely without the second. The practical man has much of the second kind but has a very slight hold on the first. And so neither of them is wise or capable of making wise decisions.

Let us look further at this knowledge of particulars, for it is easily confused with practical knowledge. The understanding of particular men, events and situations consists in part, but only in part, in focusing as much theoretical or scientific knowledge as possible on the particular thing under investigation. Since no single thing, person, situation or event is exactly the same as any other, the "constellation" of the items of truth that you will discover about this thing will be unique. You will know then in what ways this thing is different from every other thing. Much of this process of sizing up a situation or person or event will require the exercise of Pascal's *esprit de finesse,* the activity of the mind that tries to comprehend at once all the myriad relations and modes of inference—causal, logical, historical, associational, definitional—that help to make the particular thing understood.

But there will also be needed an *acquaintance* with the thing to be known, a way of knowing that goes deeper into the heart of the thing than any science or keen perception can go. And in addition to this there must be an evaluation which estimates the relative importance of the elements in the situation and (if the situation is a human one) the moral position and responsibility of every person concerned. All this is necessary if a person is really to understand a man, a thing, a situation or an event. And all this must be present in an operative and applicable way if a person is to be able to decide wisely when faced by the problems that arise in the world.

Our higher education as it is carried on at present is failing because it leads young people to fragments of truth only, but it is failing perhaps even more disastrously in that it makes almost no effort to lead them to this most necessary knowledge of particulars. Is it possible to devise a form of higher education for our youth which will lead them to see the splendor of the whole of truth—truth in ideas and truth in particular things, truth in values and truth in actions? If we can do this we may have a plan of education that leads to wisdom.

First let us see how the potentiality of such a plan once existed in our tradition, and how it was lost.

* * *

3

Every human community has had its kind of higher education, its way of handing on to chosen ones of the next generation the truths and values that it holds to be important: a knowledge of the world and how to get along in it, a knowledge of the community's past and its ideals, a knowledge of its skills and secrets. The selected ones are expected to become the wise men by whom the vital decisions of the community are made.

The forms of this higher education—the ways in which what is valued has been handed down the generations—have been many.

One of these forms is poetry—the epic style as well as others—the songs which celebrate the marvelous deeds of the men of ancient time contain also a compendium of all the manifold truth that the community cherishes. The songs are learned, recited and lovingly contemplated by the young student so that they will be for him a constant source both of inspiration and of reference—both Bible and encyclopedia.

Another source of higher learning is the collected sayings of the elders, which are studied and memorized by the young. Still another is an original deposit of divine revelation handed down from generation to generation. Knowledge transmitted in all these ways grows by the comments of its more or less official custodians, but it is not supposed to change fundamentally. Accuracy of transmission is insisted upon, and the body of knowledge remains a massive and venerable structure unless something happens to make the community reject it altogether.

In all these ways of handing down the intellectual heritage there is a constant relation between the older and younger generations. The older generation hands out; the younger receives. Sitting at the feet of the elder is the proper attitude of the learner. Complete respect is what he owes the teacher.

In the intellectual tradition we call Western, however, there is, along with the above-mentioned elements and attitudes and often overshadowing them, a unique way of educating: a discussion or dialogue in which there is a certain tension between teacher and learner. The teacher does not simply hand out, and the learner does not simply take. There is not simply a body of truth to be handed down. Instead, what is presented is presented problematically. Teacher and learner both confront the problem, contributing to its solution by the positive assertion of a position, or by criticizing what the other has proposed. Education here comes from participating in the dialogue. The difference between teacher and learner is only relative, the teacher being one who is more experienced in the world and in the dialogue, the learner being a kind of apprentice who, as he becomes experienced, will be able to teach in his turn.

The dialogue goes on through the years, developing new content by discovery and by criticism, extending its range and shifting its emphasis as successive generations of teachers and learners enter and retire from it. It is a school always in session. The generations participating in the dialogue at any one time constitute *a community of learning, a community in which the desire to know is the driving force and whose pedagogical method is the drawing of the beginner into the intellectual life of the community so that the desire to know becomes progressively satisfied and in being satisfied is further stimulated.*

This dialogue is not at all an example of the "togetherness" so much prized by the apostles of group dynamics. The actual dialogue is not so much the *milieu* in which discovery is made as the *milieu* in which individuals receive their inspiration to investigate and in which their discoveries are examined. The discovery itself is most often made in solitude, by research or by contemplation, and is then brought to the dialogue to be criticized and to be added in its corrected form to the body of already existing knowledge. Thus the participant in the dialogue alternately withdraws from it into solitude and re-enters it with something new to contribute.

When Christianity came into the Greco-Roman world the dialogue had already been going on for some centuries. The elements of Christian revelation, themselves gained not at all by a dialectic process, were taken into the discussion as new data, to illumine the already existing content of knowledge and to be illumined by it. Thus there arose the science of theology.

The central learning process of the Western tradition has been the dialogue. This fact is responsible for much of the good in our tradition.

One of these characteristics of the dialogue is the important role of criticism. Since there is a tension often amounting to rivalry among the participants, each is eager to find the weak point in the position of the other end to make his own position stronger. Every position is subject to examination by keen minds; no position can be simply asserted with no attempt at rational support. All who take part in the dialogue must be alert constantly. And because of this situation a new element enters the educational ideal: *Besides handing down valued knowledge, education should develop the intellect of the learner.* The learner is supposed to become not only a repository of knowledge but a man who can think, criticize and discover.

This same tension also accounts for the dynamic character of the Western tradition. Participants in the dialogue are always seeking something new, either to refute an opponent, bolster a position, or follow an avenue of investigation. There is no "this is the last word that can be spoken" idea. There is a premium placed upon discovery and upon the flights of imagination leading to it. Every line of development has an infinite possibility of extension. There is no forbidden field.

It is the fact of the dialogue rather than any particular racial characteristic or technical skill of Europeans that has prevented the Western tradition from remaining static. The Chinese, it is said, had a navigational technique in the Middle Ages that was far superior to anything in Europe, but they did not have among their learned men a fierce argument as to whether the earth was circumnavigable, an argument which could be settled only by trying to circumnavigate it.

This same fact of the dialogue accounts also for the peculiar kind of unity found in our tradition, a unity not of intellectual agreement but of mutual understanding and communication between even violently disagreeing parties. We have never been unanimous in our beliefs, but where the dialogue has been maintained we have understood our opponents' positions and have argued about them. We have not, where the dialogue has existed, built a wall of separation between the convictions which different groups of us have maintained.

The integration which has existed in this exciting, fruitful, but precarious tradition has been one of communication and understanding rather than one of system or point of view. The Platonist has been willing to talk with the Aristotelian, even if only to disagree with him. The Stoic would converse with the Epicurean. They were all participants in the one dialogue. The natural exclusiveness of each intellectual could not keep out of the dialogue the views of other intellectuals who differed from him completely, because the dialogue was public and general. All points of view could get a hearing. The elasticity of the tradition was well shown in the thirteenth century, when the supposedly atheistic Aristotelianism of the Arabs, together with their Ptolemaic astornomy, was welcomed and absorbed despite the protests of the more conservative theologians, and began to redirect the whole thinking of the dialogue.

This dialogue, as the central means of higher education, did more than enlarge the minds of its participants by leading them to consider all subjects presented for discussion. It made their minds extraordinarily agile in focusing all their knowledge and all their skill on the particular point at issue.

The great dialogue, then, has been the traditional means of Western higher education. It has also been, in the past, the environment in which and because of which our knowledge has advanced. Because of it our very diverse fields of knowledge and our very diverse opinions have been so integrated as to be parts of one cultural heritage. Where the dialogue has been maintained we have had real intellectual unity in spite of the centrifugal tendencies of the intellectual life. We have not agreed on many things, but we have understood each other. And among all the specializations and concentrations of interest there has been, where the dialogue has been maintained, *a certain very minimal agreement,* a certain public philosophy, containing fundamental truths about the great things to be known: God, man, human society and the world. This was a real philosophy, a set of reasoned convictions—reasoned because discussed and argued out in every generation in the dialogue. And further, the loss of this public philosophy, so deeply lamented by Mr. Walter Lippman, has not come about because of disproof. We have lost this public philosophy because most people have become totally unfamiliar with the way it had been argued satisfactorily in the dialogue. A whole way of knowing, because of our interest in other things, has escaped our knowledge. Wherever and whenever the dialogue has been impeded, or people have been educated outside its environment, integration of knowledge, appreciation of all the ways of knowing, and mutual understanding among thinkers, all have disappeared.

We are at present in an age where the dialogue is not functioning at the highest level, although there are many subordinate dialogues going on. We are finding it progressively more difficult to talk to one another. There seems at first sight to be little common ground between us, say, and the men of the Marxian tradition. But the lack of communication exists at home, too. Attention has lately been called to the fact that in our society there are two cultures that can scarcely communicate with each other: the culture of science and the culture of the humanities. We have mentioned already that this is an overoptimistic view of the situation, that in actuality there are at least three of these mutually exclusive thought-worlds dividing our intellectuals and our society.

This situation has been brought about not by any great increase of knowledge, as has often been supposed, but to a large extent because our higher education and our higher educators, the scholars, have been separated from the dialogue. The separation has been intellectual, moral, and institutional. Just as our ancestors in the Western tradition built for themselves institutions in which the dialogue could prosper (e.g. the ancient schools in Athens and in Alexandria, and medieval universities) so our modern intellectuals have built for themselves and for us institutions of learning which by their ideals and their structure prevent the dialogue from taking place.

The intellectual separation of thinkers from the institutions where the dialogue was going on can be detected at least as early as the Renaissance. The universities, grown old and stiff, refused to take into their midst the new ideas and enthusiasms connected with the classical revival and with the heightened interest in the beautiful. The dialogue which was the life of the universities was thus deprived of many new inspirations which might have broadened and refreshed it; and the representatives of the new interests, with all their earnestness, ability and vivid imagination, increased and multiplied altogether without benefit of the refined wisdom of the tradition and without the interchange of understanding which could have channeled their new learning into one stream with the old philosophy.

It was the same with the founders of the new science. The custodians of the dialogue in the sixteenth and seventeenth centuries, having lost the experimental attitude of their predecessors who had been able to take in the newly rediscovered thought of Aristotle and make it their own, were now completely unwilling to give a hearing either to the findings or to the methods of the new experimenters. And so the new school of experimental science grew up in almost complete isolation from the wisdom of the past and with a rather determined prejudice against it.

Of course the representatives of the new science were not completely free from old prejudices, and their successors had good grounds for complaint against the conservatism of their predecessors. Descartes was still a scholastic in many ways. He assumed the validity of the principle of causality and used it to erect his rationalist system which so irritated the empiricists. And Galileo's devotion to the perfect circles of Plato made him unwilling to accept the elliptical orbits of the planets.

But the scientific innovators, disagreeing with one another in many things, were united in their contempt for the old learning. They understood it no more than its representatives understood them. Thus the dialogue again lost the opportunity of extending and enriching itself, and we have two growing bodies of new knowledge—the humanities and the natural sciences—undergoing their development quite apart from any integration with the past, and thus quite narrow in their understanding, however widely their perimeter might extend. For we must insist, in spite of the present popularity of these two thought-worlds, that their dismissal of the theological, metaphysical and ethical thought of the ancient and medieval worlds constitutes a deep and essential narrowness.

The traditional dialogue, deprived of the new blood necessary for its vitality, has so sunk beneath the popularity of its rivals as to be practically insignificant as an effective means of educating men.

Our ancestral habit of learning by dialogue survives, it is true. Both the humanities and the sciences use the method, at least in their advanced circles. But it is a mutilated dialogue that they use, a dialogue completely failing in the most valuable function of taking people out of their own field and forcing them, as it were, to look seriously at what is outside. The humanists and the scientists discuss and argue with one another in their own separate fields, neither group trespassing on the territory of the other except perhaps to sneer, and neither of them considering the great truths discovered and maintained in the old dialogue.

And because the great dialogue no longer exists as a means of integration and intercommunication, thinkers no longer simply disagree with one another. They do not understand each other. They do not speak to one another. Thus our thought-world is so broken up that we are no longer members of one culture. The humanist and the scientist, separated from each other, are also separated from the realm of metaphysics, ethics and theology, so that they are not even able to evaluate the knowledge that they themselves possess. The imaginative writer as such is no more conversant with our ethical tradition than is the physicist as such, and neither of them can give a good account of what they mean by reality and of the relation of their knowledge to it.

This lack of a common cultural ground is disastrous from an intellectual point of view in that it prevents any integration of knowledge. But it is a catastrophe also from the social and political point of view in that it makes impossible that agreement on fundamental convictions upon which a united community must be based.

Walter Lippman in his *The Public Philosophy* has shown the fact of this disappearance and its serious consequences. When common belief evaporates, the possibility of common action, after a time, disappears also.

A certain cultural integration is absolutely necessary for the maintenance of a community in any way other than by the constant use of force; and if such an integration, in an intellectually active people, is brought about and secured by the existence of a genuine dialogue, then the re-establishment of this dialogue in an effective way through effective institutions is essential for the continuance of our community. Since this re-establishment will be for the purpose of educating people, and especially people who will be leaders, the institutions will be institutions of higher education.

The dialogue must be *effective*. This means that it cannot be simply a reproduction of the ancient or medieval dialogue. The ancient and medieval schools, through unavoidable ignorance, did not include in their discussion the richness of Oriental thought. The modern dialogue must incorporate it. The Greek tradition of interest in the universal and contempt for the particular directed the attention of the old schools almost entirely to ideas and their relationships, and the schools in consequence produced the student who was academic. The modern dialogue must be so directed as to enable its members to understand the particular thing, person and situation, and so to understand the world in which they are to be leaders.

We come now to the principal purpose of this book: a discussion of the kind of educational institution in which an effective dialogue can be established and maintained. If what we have said about the dialogue has any truth, this is one of the most important problems in the whole field of higher education.

There is no lack of plans among us for the reform of higher education. But most of the reformers are prisoners in the modern educational tradition. They think in terms of courses, departments, specializations and "raising standards." They are scholars, for whom competence in a field is the breath of life; or, something much worse, they are administrators who believe that by the proper manipulation of men and money *they* can bring about a situation in which young people will come to know what is worth knowing.

25

But if the fundamental tendencies in the modern educational world are wrong in having led to the disruption of the unity of knowledge, in having splintered the truth, then the people—scholars and administrators—who have attained eminence in the educational world as it is are the most unlikely people in the world to bring about a thorough-going educational reform. They are efficient leaders leading in the wrong direction, and the more successful they are, the farther along the wrong road education finds itself.

One might state as a historical generalization that those men who bring about a radical improvement in an existing situation do not come from among those who are eminent in that situation. The men who introduced the new physics in the seventeenth century did not come from among the old Aristotelian physicists. Not many of the founding fathers of the United States came from the ranks of the office holders under the royal government. If this generalization holds, the government and the philanthropic foundations are doomed to failure in their efforts to reform education as long as they take for their advisors and consultants men who are eminent in the present educational regime.

In this book therefore I would like to appeal over the heads of the professional educators—scholars and administrators—to the people who want to be really educated, to the people who expect educated people to be leaders, and most of all to the people who are now in the educational profession and who see themselves so hemmed in by the irrelevant requirements of scholarship and administration that they are continually being prevented from carrying out their vocation as teachers of human beings.

* * *

4

We have asked if it is possible to design a form of higher education which will enable the student to begin to grasp the whole unsplintered splendor of truth, so that a foundation of wisdom may be laid. We have seen how our Western tradition of learning through dialogue has furnished a method by which people can come to understand and appreciate different ways of knowing, come in contact with the great realities to be known, and have their intellects sharpened for further discovery and for ever deeper appreciation.

What we must do, then, is to design an educational institution in which young people can be drawn into an intensive and extensive dialogue for a few years, at the time when their minds are opening to the wonder of knowing, before they enter into the specialization which seems to be inevitable for most people in the modern world. We must not think that in designing such an institution we are preparing these young people for specialization in the sense that our purpose is to make them better specialists. Our purpose is to prepare them by protecting them against the dangers that accompany specialization.

If a man expects to enter an occupation in which he will spend most of his time sitting down, the teacher who has charge of his physical training does not ask himself, "How can I train this man so that he will be a good 'sitter-downer'?" He asks rather, "How can I train this man so that his body can withstand the dangers of sedentary life? How can I give him such a love of exercise that he will use his leisure time for something besides sitting down?"

The physicist, if he is only a physicist, is a mental "sitter-downer," no matter how nuclear he may become. He is using his mind from one position only, no matter how extensively and how skillfully he may be using it. His constant maintenance of that one mental position is abnormal, unhealthy. It leads to a hardening of the mental arteries.

The real higher education of men, higher in the sense of being more important to them as human beings, has as its purpose the training of their minds into full health, so that if and when they specialize they will be able to withstand the dangers inherent in an abnormal way of mental life. The specialist-to-be needs this training more than anyone else, because he more than anyone else will be subject to the tensions of an abnormal mental life. Subsequent training in a specialty is not higher education but merely later education; and unless the mind is healthy it will restrict the intellect's elasticity and deaden its responses.

True higher education must aim at some fundamental knowing of all the great realities that can be known, and at a familiarity with all the ways in which these realities can be known, so that the student can perfect himself as far as possible as a knower of the things that are and as an understander of the situations in which he finds himself—in short, as a man of wisdom.

In designing an educational institution which will have some prospect of accomplishing all this, we must forget for a time all that we think of in connection with our conventional idea of "college" or "university." We must not be fettered by what is being done, by what educators think, by what people want, by what people will stand for, or by what wealthy men will give money for. We must not even be bound by what accrediting agencies will approve of. Forget for the moment all ideas of courses and credits, of departments and deans, of instructors and professors, of grades and diplomas, of presidents and boards of trustees, and think only of this: what form of institution will be best for the genuine higher education of young people? This institution does not have to be like any institution that ever was. It has only to be the best. If no one wants it now, that should make no difference in our planning. We should design the most perfect institution possible, so that when some one does want it the plans will be there.

The essential element in our institution of higher learning will not be a campus or a set of buildings or an administration. The essential element is *a group of persons among whom the process of teaching and learning is going on.* The educational process is personal; it is a complex of relations between human beings. The structure of our institution must above all else allow and encourage these complex personal relations to function freely and well. No administration with its own peculiar requirements, no equipment, no extraneous demands of any kind must be allowed to interfere with this functioning.

There will be a loose distinction, within this group of persons, between those who are willing and able to teach and those who are willing and able to learn. The distinction is only loose, because the teachers will also be learning all the time in their contact with the learners and in their private and corporate search for truth; and the learners will be sharing with one another and with the teachers the truth as it dawns on them, and thus will be teachers. The teachers will be distinguished from the learners rather as elder brothers are distinguished from younger—by the fact that they have presumably had more experience in the vocation of knowing and therefore would more often be in the position of leaders in the intellectual life of the group. But whenever one of the younger brothers has something of value to offer, he for the moment becomes leader and all learn from him.

This group of teachers and learners can well be called a community because there will be in all its members one unifying purpose: the desire to know and to understand, and to share this knowledge and understanding with all the fellowship. It is a community of learning.

In this community those called teachers will constitute the more or less permanent element. They are the enduring core of the community, and they themselves, prior to the addition of those called learners, must constitute a fellowship where the intellectual dialogue is going on with intensity. These teachers, in addition to whatever interest they may have in one special field of knowledge, must have that same respect for, and interest in, all the ways of knowing that they expect the learners to attain, and they must be eager to know and understand more all the time. They must exist as a living intellectual community—a going concern—before any students join them, so that the students as

29

they arrive will become members of an already functioning organism.

The education of the student will primarily consist in his being drawn into this community of learning so that he gradually becomes partaker of its life and receives the imprint of it. He will be introduced by his teachers and fellow learners to the different things to be known and the different ways of knowing them; and each acquirement will lead him farther into the intellectual life of the community so that he increasingly takes part in the dialogue. Each thing he learns, and each skill or liberal art that he acquires comes to be used in the dialogue, so that the knowledge and the skill are constantly exercised. In this situation a forgotten fact, an obscure date, are not laboriously recalled for purposes of examination. On the contrary, each concept and each ability is kept new through use, and at the end of the period of college education all that the student has learned is at his finger tips, every part of it more at his command than, while first learning it, he paid special attention to it.

In this community the chief incentive to learning will not be grades with the prospect of a degree, or threats with a prospect of failure. It will be the desire of the student himself to take part fully in the life of the community. A person who does not want to learn will be excluded from this vivid life around him, and he will either come to want to learn so that he can enter it, or he will leave the institution. We must remember that the students and teachers together constitute this community and that the student as he is drawn into it comes into fellowship with both. In so far as he is excluded by his unwillingness to think and learn, he is excluded from fellowship with the other students as well as with the teachers. There will be no substitute fellowship of sports to offer him an alternative home within the institution. If he doesn't know what the students and teachers are talking about in their discussions, their jokes, their arguments and their bull-sessions he can't very well be one of them. If he wants to be one of them he will have to strive to be able to enter the dialogue.

A superficial fluency is not what is meant by "taking full part in the dialogue." I have in mind a seminar in which a silent and retiring student established himself at the center of the dialogue, and in the respect of his teacher and fellow students, *by asking one question,* but a question so devastating to the gabby people and so revealing of the knowledge and wisdom of the man who asked it that no more was needed. It is not the fluent people who are admitted to the inner circle of this fellowship; it is the people whose minds are respected. The community is quick to take the measure of a man's emptiness.

The attraction of being admitted into the comradeship of the community of learning, then, is an educative force which, for people who are at an age when they can begin to value ideas, is more effective than any threat, or any promise of such an extrinsic reward as a high grade or a degree. It is a force which could lead men to think and to learn even if there were no professional teachers in the community.

Let me give an example of this kind of comradely community of learning which we find flourishing in many of our American colleges and universities. I mean the way in which the art and science of football is learned. The student when he enters college finds that he has joined a community of people who have a consuming interest to which they are eager to devote their emotions and their intellects. This interest is football. The new student may not know anything about football. He may even dislike it. But if he is to take part in the life and fellowship of his community, if he is even to talk to his neighbors, he has to learn something about it. Because of the enthusiasm of the others he finds it almost impossible not to be drawn finally into this common interest. By the time he graduates he knows football. He can talk intelligently about its by no means contemptible intricacies. He can recognize and applaud skill; and he finds himself quickened by the life that flows through the community. This man has received an education of a kind. He has been educated by being drawn into the life and comradeship of a community. He has become interested in something; he has learned about something; and he has become articulate in thinking about that something and in talking about it to his fellows.

It is to be noted that this education has been gained without benefit of professional teachers, courses, grades, examinations or degrees. No disciplinary action on the part of authority has been needed to encourage or to threaten. It might be said that in some of our colleges this football education has been more successful than the attempts at liberal and professional education which were going on in the same place at the same time, involving the same students, and with the support of the official apparatus of the college. The school has functioned better in the teaching and learning of football than in the teaching and learning of anything else. Why has this been so? It has happened because in the subjects set forth in the catalogue no community of learning has been established, while in the subject of football the students and some of the teachers have spontaneously set up such a community. *The community is the fundamental means of educating young people who are of an age to think.*

An institution which is to teach such people must have as its principal intention the setting up of such a community as the basic activity around which all its other educational activities are to be gathered. All administrative considerations and all considerations of professional scholarship must yield to this fundamental purpose. The other educational activities will supply the student with materials to equip him for entering the fellowship where he can develop them, co-ordinate them and put them together in the dialogue and thus become a more educated man.

By these other activities I mean all those ways which men have devised to help along the process of teaching and learning: lectures, "recitations," private tuition of students, discussions between students and teachers, assigned readings and writings, laboratory experiments, co-operative projects among students, spontaneous investigations, solitary meditation and contemplation, seminars, panel discussions, browsing in the library, and many more. In any of these ways the student may get inspiration or enlightenment or information which he can then bring *to* the dialogue for criticism and for maturation into knowledge, and in these ways also he can criticize and mature what he brings *from* the dialogue.

It must be the job of the teachers to see that these means of learning are always available to the student and that he is encouraged to try them out so that he can see which ones are useful to *him*. But they must never be considered ends in themselves so

32

that the student is "graded" according to his use of them or his success in this use. They are to be regarded simply as ways in which the student can be helped to take a fuller part in the intellectual life of the community. If he can take part without using some of them, or if he can devise ways of his own that work better for him, well and good. *That he should think, and that by thinking he should learn and grow in wisdom, that he should be able to use his knowledge in the understanding of what is worthy of being understood, and that he should share what he has gained with the other members of the community—this is what is expected of the student, and it is on his success in this enterprise alone that any meaningful grade can be given.*

If all these ways of imparting knowledge, usually considered to be the very core of the educational process, are here considered only peripheral, in what will the central means of education, the dialogue, consist? How is the life of the community of learning to be carried on? What specific process can contain the actuality of this life? What happens at a certain time and place which leads a person to say, "There the dialogue is going on"? These are valid questions.

The dialogue will have both its formal and its informal phases.

The formal dialogue will take place at stated regular times. The teachers and students will meet together as a body for the discussion of a specific subject. A thesis will be proposed, a report given, a question raised or a poem read by someone, teacher or student or visitor, who has been thinking seriously about it. Then what has been presented will be discussed. This dialogue must not be a "stage play" put on for the students. The discussion must take place with perfect honesty, each person doing his best to reach the truth. There must be no attempt to bring the discussion to the level of the most ignorant student, but there *must* be an attempt to make it as clear as the nature of the subject permits. And respectful attention must be paid to what the most ignorant student may say or ask.

These discussions should be varied so as to take in, say in the course of a year or two, a consideration of the great mathematical, historical, political and philosophical realities to be known and the different ways of knowing them. Whenever there is op-

33

portunity, men from outside the institution should be invited to present something for discussion. These should include not only acedemic persons, but politicians and business men, farmers and woodsmen, union men, religious leaders, writers, artists, and uneducated men who are articulate, so that the dialogue in the college may maintain contact with the world and that fresh air may blow in upon the academic tradition.

This great attention paid to visitors will provide for our necessarily small community the advantage of coming into contact with many points of view, an advantage often praised by those favoring large educational institutions.

The important thing is that this formal dialogue be regarded as a central activity of the community, an activity in which all the teachers and students are to take part. It should take place, say, on one evening a week, and nothing else should be scheduled to interfere with it. The burden of choosing the subjects to be discussed in this dialogue, and for keeping the thing going, will of course fall on the teachers. This formal dialogue will also occasionally allow the teacher to bring before the public the results of his private thought and investigation. He will thus make the whole community aware of his accomplishments (or, unhappily, his lack of them); he will profit by the criticisms and suggestions of his fellows, and he will contribute to the content of the dialogue. Educationally this practice will be much more to the point than the present practice of "publishing" for an audience quite outside the community and quite distinct from the people whom the publisher is supposed to be teaching.

There will be opportunity in these public discussions for the students to be given a hearing before the whole community. If a student has made a discovery, if he has thought of a new explanation, if he has a good criticism to make, he can present it for formal consideration. We have said that the distinction between teachers and students will be a loose one in our community. By means of this public discussion true intellectual achievement will reveal itself. If a student is superior to some of his teachers or to all of his teachers, the fact will appear. Each man can take the position that he deserves in the respect of the community. And each man, student or official teacher, can also take the rank that he deserves in teaching, for when the intellectual stature of every man is known, those who wish to learn can go to the one who knows, whether he is a teacher or a student.

The formal dialogue will be perhaps the most effective means of forming the persons in the institution into one community. It will be the best agency for counteracting the centrifugal tendencies of the intellectual life. In it people will come to know and understand each other even though they disagree. It can provide for the community on a small scale what the great dialogue in the past supplied to our Western tradition: the one kind of unity to which intellectually active persons can submit. In most of our contemporary institutions of higher learning men get farther and farther apart when they think, and they come together as a community only at a football game or when fighting with the administration about salaries.

What is to be discussed in the formal dialogue? Anything that constitutes a serious intellectual problem. Here are some samples, problems which have been discussed fruitfully in a group composed of teachers and students: What is a cause in history? What is the intellectual status of an economic law such as the law of supply and demand? What is the basis of communication between human beings and animals? Is disinterested love possible? Is there any difference between what is right and what is customary? Can we find a definition of *conservative* and *liberal* which will be acceptable both to conservatives and liberals?

It is possible for a community of teachers and students to get really excited about problems such as these. I have seen a group of football players aroused almost to the fighting stage over the question of whether or not man has an inborn esthetic sense.

To raise such questions in public discussion is not of course to find pat answers. But the discussion does stretch the students' intellects. It lets them see phases of problems and even whole problems that they never thought of before. It gives them experience in many different ways of thinking. It gives them the material for solving in their own minds, for themselves, problems which the public dialogue does not solve for everybody. And, as one professor said to me, it enables even the youngest students to distinguish between important and unimportant questions.

35

The *informal* phase of the dialogue will be taking place all the time, wherever and whenever members of the community get together. If the discussion of the formal dialogue has been interesting it will be continued with spirit when students or teachers meet. Students who are studying the same thing will naturally come together to talk about their subjects. Where students and teachers meet to eat or drink or smoke conversation will begin. There is no need whatever that this informal discussion should be on a low level. That it usually is so now means that most of our schools have failed to establish a high intellectual interest among their students. There is plenty of evidence to show that young people are just as willing to talk about the nature of a triangle as about basketball.

In our school the informal dialogue will be continually enriched by visitors to the community. They will make their formal presentation of their subject in the formal dialogue, but they will be encouraged to stay around for a while, sometimes even for several days, to talk to the students. Indeed, if a visitor should come who has something to say or to do that is worth while—an artist or a statesman for instance—the community might decide to suspend all scheduled activities for a few days in order to make the best use of his presence.

I remember an instance of this kind in a small school several years ago. We were visited by a physicist who was also a doctor of music. He had been a pupil of Einstein's. For a week we did nothing but listen to him, talk with him, argue with him and entertain him. Never was a week more profitably spent. At the formal seminars he talked about the relationships between physics and music, but informally we talked about everything. We got the views of a physicist on philosophical, religious and historical questions. (He had escaped from the Nazis.) We heard stories of Einstein and his ideas about the use of the imagination in scientific investigation. At the end we were not physicists or musicians. We were not trying to be. But we did have a much greater respect for what the physicist and the musician were doing. And, as he wrote afterwards, our physicist also learned something in that week that he spent with us.

Through the dialogue, formal and informal, the student comes to know without having his knowledge divided into compartments. His knowledge remains a unity while growing within him; and while his own knowledge is growing, that of his fellow students and his teachers grows too. He is developing his mind in an environment where there has been constant communication between people of various interests and various talents. Moreover, this knowledge of his has been in constant use in the course of its acquisition, for in the dialogue he has been learning to bring it all to bear on the particular point at issue. His mind will never be compartmentalized. Neither will any of its functions grow rusty from lack of use.

The quiet, retiring student will profit just as much from the dialogue as will the fluent one, but in a different way. By being present and seeing what is going on he will be helped to integrate in his own mind what he is learning. He may be taking it all in even though he may be saying almost nothing. He may have no love whatever for plunging into discussion. He may shrink from the competitive contact of mind with mind. This is quite all right. He need not do this thing that he loathes; but he needs the intellectual broadening his own mind will get if he is present when others are doing it. No man's intellect can be wide if it develops in isolation, just as no man's intellect can be deep if it develops only in a social setting. All men need solitude and all men need the dialogue.

Neither is the dialogue of value only for the superior student. The man of average or less than average intelligence can profit by hearing things discussed on levels that he himself finds it almost impossible to reach, and often under these conditions such a man will reveal an intellectual capacity which no one, least of all the man himself, suspected. And he will develop a maturity of mind that will give him a wisdom beyond what is usual for a person of his intellectual attainments.

I remember one student who made this plea as he applied for admission into a program where the dialogue was going on: He was failing where he was, and if he was going to fail he wanted to fail where something worth while was going on. This man said to me much later that it was his experience in the dialogue that kept him sane during his life in the army. It had given him something worth while to think about, while most of his fellows were concerned chiefly with women and alcohol.

The opportunity of being present while brilliant people discuss what he himself is trying to learn is a privilege for the ordinary student even when he has a hard time understanding what is said. But the presence of quite ordinary people in the community of learning is also a great privilege for the brilliant man. He learns not only courtesy and forebearance. He is compelled to express his ideas so that the ordinary man can begin to grasp them or, if he cannot do that, he must come to see at what point this man has lost contact.

There is no better way to see inconsistencies in one's own theory than to try to explain it to a very ordinary man who is studying the same thing. There is great insight in the words of the late Peter Maurin, author of *Easy Essays,* who said that he took the high-brow stuff and put it in low-brow language so that the high brows could understand it. The brilliant man receives a valuable education by mingling with ordinary men in the community of learning.

In the formal dialogue the problems discussed will usually not be practical problems. We would not deliberate, for example, on how to get better meals for less money. We would discuss problems of being and knowing—what a thing is and how it is known. There are great realities to be known and many ways of knowing each of them. It is in this area that our intellectual problems are to be found. God, man, human society and the physical universe—these are the things that are, and are to be studied. And these are the important ways of knowing: the way of mathematics, the way of metaphysics, the way of natural science, the way of history, the way of ethics, the way of art, and the way of faith. It is extremely important that in the formal dialogue none of these realities or ways of knowing be slighted. The student must be accustomed to serious discussion of all of them. A program must be made out so that no one of them will be neglected too long.

In the informal dialogue, of course, no program can be planned, for the discussion is spontaneous, but here also an effort must be made by the teachers and senior students to initiate informal discussions of the problems that are being neglected. If the discussion of such a problem in the formal dialogue has been exciting, there will inevitably follow much exciting discussion in private, so that the neglected subject will be taken care of.

What is to be the life of the student in this community of learning? He spends one evening a week in the formal dialogue. He spends much time discussing things in the informal dialogue. But what does he do the rest of the time? Just how are his studies pursued?

When the student enters, a teacher will plot out a course of study for him which is designed to give him a systematic acquaintance with the things to be known and the ways of knowing them. This course of study will make use of all the ways of learning we mentioned earlier which may be available at the time. The student will be directed to courses of lectures that will be given. He will spend much time in assigned reading. He will do much assigned writing. As the student advances he will be allowed more and more to make his own plan of study, for if he does not soon learn self-discipline in study he will be better off outside the community of learning.

This community, since it is a community of persons, and since teaching and learning are such thoroughly human relationships between persons, will be very careful to avoid the great American sin of premature and superfluous organization. We like to set up a completely worked-out system of education beforehand, and then require teachers and students to conform to it. But this is fatal to any genuinely human activity. The student and the teacher are both of them unique persons. The relationship between any one teacher and any one student is also unique and cannot profitably be forced into uniformity with any other teacher-student relationship. Therefore any general plan of study must be exceedingly flexible so that it can be adapted to each case. The community furnishes the means of education, and makes them as varied as is possible with its resources. The teacher and the student together, and later the student alone, must decide how these means are best to be made use of.

But, I repeat, the dialogue is the great means of education, for both students and teachers. The results of the student's course of study are the materials which are brought to the dialogue to be tested and matured, supplemented, corrected and forged into wisdom.

While teachers and learners will constitute the central and essential persons in the community of learning, there may be other persons as well. The retired scholar, for instance, who does not wish to do any official teaching, can simply by being present, carrying on his studies, talking to people about what he is doing, and once in a while attending the formal dialogue, be a real help to the students and the teachers. The artist in residence, concerned more with his art than with the teaching of it, would be a wonderful addition to the community if only people could occasionally watch him at his work and talk with him about it. Such men, who do not wish to participate fully in what the community is doing but who have interests and occupations related to the chief interests of the community, would be welcomed. Their advice would be sought, but they would not have a voice in the government of the community. Only the teachers and the students would make decisions directing community life.

As the community continues it would probably enroll a certain number of people like these, who are neither teachers nor students but who for one personal reason or another have found a place for themselves there. The fact that the institution has only the minimum of organization will make it easier for these men to find a place even though there is no organizational pigeonhole for them.

In our community of learning as we have described it so far, what goes on bears at least some resemblance to what goes on in a conventional college. The likeness is close enough to allow us to call our community a college, and we shall do so from time to time. But what follows will be far different from what is usually considered higher education. It is needed, however, if the education is to be really higher; that is, if it is to lead the students to the completion of knowing.

* * *

5

Our community of learning, if it is truly to be an institution of higher learning, must also be a community where understanding takes place.

This conception of understanding as a completion of knowing has been mentioned before, and now needs some further working out. We hope that our meaning of understanding will become clear as we proceed. The word is used here not in any of its technical philosophical meanings, but in its popular meaning as the successful completion of the process of knowing something. Understanding, in its popular usage, is the best word that can be used to describe our knowing. When you understand something you *really* know it. The act of finding out has reached a satisfactory terminus.

Our educators have been academic (that is, Greek) in their point of view, and our schools, in their most successful moments, have consequently produced academic knowers. But they have not produced understanders. And since leadership requires understanding, the outstanding knowers sent out by our colleges have not been leaders.

From the study of things and reflection on self the human race has produced in its tradition the body of ideas that we call knowledge. Our Western tradition contains not only a very large body of knowledge, but contains it in the form of *sciences,* great organized *systems* of knowledge relating to the various aspects of reality. The ideas contained in each system of science are joined by a distinct set of relations. For the Greeks, who were largely responsible for constructing these sciences, higher education consisted in coming to know them. Contemplation of the ordered universal truth—that is, of the ideas systematically related to one

41

another—was the highest activity of the intellect. The interest of a perfect man should be in this realm of ideas, to think of them, to love them, and if possible to extend man's knowledge of them. This perfect man is what we would now call the academic man.

Our educators have been quite critical of this academic ideal as the goal of higher education, but they have nevertheless put it into practice almost everywhere. Knowledge of a science is almost everywhere the desired result of the teaching of that science. Where will you find a class in biology, for instance, in which a student will be graded "unsatisfactory" if all that he attains in the class is a good knowledge of the science of biology? (The very fact that the reader may at this point feel quite bewildered at such a question shows that he too has accepted the academic ideal of education, perhaps without thinking much about it.)

But to regard the knowledge of a science as a final point in a learning process is, except in the case of mathematical science, to leave the process incomplete, poised in the air as it were. What do you mean when you say, "I know biology"? Biology is an organized body of knowledge about living things. When I know biology, then, I know a body of knowledge. This bare statement, "I know a body of knowledge" means "I am acquainted with a system of ideas." But this system of ideas has been built up in the past by the *investigation of something*. It is a set of truths *about something*. It is one of the ways in which that *something* may be known. Now if I focus my attention in learning upon that set of truths *as a system*, I can easily forget (or I may never even realize) that they are truths about something. I can fail altogether to turn my attention to that something, *and can fail to understand it even though I am familiar with the truths as a system*. A person can know biology and can at the same time be almost totally ignorant of the living things around him.

I have excepted mathematics from what I have said concerning the incompleteness of scientific knowledge as such, for the realities that the mathematical sciences are *about* are the ideas themselves and certain of their relations. In mathematics the science itself is the final goal of learning, the terminus of the knowing process. Therefore in mathematics the purely academic ideal is perfectly satisfactory. But the other sciences are about something other than themselves and are *not* the terminus of the knowing process. If, in studying biology, the student is satisfied when he has come to know the science well, and does not use that scientific knowledge to help him understand the living things around him, the result of the process has been unsatisfactory.

Every man finds himself in a bewildering welter of particular but related things, persons, situations and events with which he has to deal in some way. In order to deal with them intelligently he must understand them as far as he can, and if he has the normal desire to know, he wants also to understand them just for the sake of understanding them. This understanding and appreciation of what is around one is a goal of human knowing which the Greeks held in little regard. But besides being of great practical value this understanding and appreciation is in itself a goal of knowing just as noble and worth-while as is science. There are men who try to understand things without any knowledge of the sciences about the things, but this is a short cut, and the resulting understanding has great gaps in it. There are also men following the Greek ideal who know the sciences but are not at all interested in the things of which the sciences are a partial knowledge. But this is an arresting of knowing before its completion. An understanding of the thing with the help of the science is a more perfect and complete act of knowing than is either the knowing of the science by itself or an attempt to understand the thing without the science.

An institution of higher learning should help men attain this more complete knowing which is understanding. It should not allow them to rest in the sciences but should teach them to focus their scientific knowledge continually on surrounding things in order to understand them. We must insist that what is meant here is not applied science as it is understood by our schools of engineering. In applied science we do indeed focus our scientific knowledge on things, but we do it in order to use them, not to understand. We are interested only in manipulating them for our purposes, and in so manipulating them we have little regard for what they are in themselves. But if knowing and not using is our aim, we want very much to know what things are in themselves.

43

We want to know it for the sake of knowing it. We want to know it so as not to be ignorant.

But the knowledge that we usually call scientific is not the only knowledge to be brought to bear in the understanding of things. Every one of the ways of knowing supplies a content, a knowledge, by the aid of which we can better understand the things around us.

To help understand a particular family, for instance, you can employ all your knowledge of the natural and social sciences. Each member of the family is a living individual with his peculiar biological constitution and his psychological make-up which can be partially understood by means of the natural sciences. The family is a social group living in a particular environment, and a further understanding of it, again partial, can be gained in the light of your knowledge of sociology and economics. But for the family and each of its members there are problems, goals and failures which can be understood only by means of a knowledge of theology, philosophy and ethics. The family also has a past and a future which are closely linked with the past and future of the larger society of which it is a part. To understand this family you must also, therefore, have a knowledge of its history and the history of the larger group. But that is not all. Examples from literature may illuminate some things about this family that you would otherwise not understand. And then, through actual acquaintance with the family, you will come to an understanding you would not get without such acquaintance.

Thus the more knowledge (and the more different kinds of knowledge) you can focus on this family, the more points of view from which you can observe it, the better you will come to understand it. But if you have not learned to focus your knowledge, you can have ever so much of it without being able to understand this particular family at all.

And it is so with the other situations, persons, events and things that you meet: all your knowledge can be of use in understanding them *if* you know how to bring it to bear; and if you do not know how to bring it to bear you can have untold amounts of it without understanding anything. Every existential situation will demand the focusing of many ways of knowing if it is to be under-

44

stood. It is only a theoretical problem that can be solved by bringing only one kind of knowledge to bear upon it.

It may be said that the college should devote its efforts to teaching theoretical knowledge—the sciences taken in their wider meaning—and leave the focusing of that knowledge on things to be acquired through later experience. Colleges have enough to do in teaching the sciences. There is no time for anything else.

But this leaving of the acts of knowing half completed—as it is when you know the theory but do not go on to understand the thing by means of the theory—is a very dangerous educational practice. The students form the habit of leaving their knowing incomplete and, if the practice is carried on long enough, they will lose interest in extending it at all. They will remain academic persons, men in an ivory tower. Many people lose in college the ability to understand persons, situations, and things. When this is true their higher education has been mis-education. They have regressed in understanding. It is this loss of the power to understand that leads people to speak of a man's being "spoiled" by his college education. We see innumerable cases, for instance, of a man coming to college from a non-intellectual environment, and as his education advances he becomes so educated away from his family and friends that he is ultimately unable to communicate with them. This separation is surely a mark of educational failure rather than success.

Our community of learning, or ideal college, must be a community which fosters in its members that completion of knowing called understanding. It must give them theory, and the ability to focus that theory on the existential situation. This will require a set of teaching and learning techniques quite novel in a college. These will have to be related to the dialogue and to the other means of education already discussed, and each will have to be allotted its proper proportion of the total time in the college course. A period of trial and error is necessary before the most satisfactory educational techniques can be worked out. Practices that look good on paper may be quite ineffective in actual use, and so far almost nothing has been done in the way of putting anything down on paper. The suggestions that follow can be only tentative, but some of them have proved effective in a very limited application.

There was a popular story in my early days by which the boys expressed their contempt for teachers in general. In an arithmetic class the teacher put this question to a boy: "If a farmer had twenty sheep in a pasture and two of them get out, how many would be left in the field?" The boy answered, "None." The teacher, of course, corrected him: "You're wrong, there would be eighteen left." The boy replied, "You may know arithmetic but you don't know sheep."

The fact that when you are making pronouncements about sheep, even declaring how many there would be in a field, you have to know sheep as well as arithmetic, illustrates a truth that so many educated people have never learned: the truth that no existential situation can be really understood by the application of one kind of knowledge alone. This is just as true and just as important as other principles used in order to know, and ways must be devised to make the students see it. The practice of teaching a certain biological truth by dissecting a cat must be supplemented by a second practice of showing the student that he really can't understand the cat by means of dissection alone. He must be kept constantly aware that in the dissecting he is learning one kind of thing about the cat, and that if he wants to understand the cat (and the cat is well worth understanding) he must try to focus as much knowledge as possible on it—on the cat as one of the *felidae*, on the cat as predator, on the cat as the embodiment of graceful movement, on the cat as a part of an ecological system, on the cat as a creature of God, and on this particular cat and its history. He must also be reminded that when he dissects a cat he thereby cuts himself off from the knowledge of that cat as a living thing. The search for one kind of knowledge sometimes makes a search for another kind of knowledge impossible unless you begin over again, and sometimes you can't begin over again. Perhaps you can't find another cat.

In the teaching-learning process the student must be constantly urged to focus whatever knowledge he is just now acquiring on the things he meets, and must be led to see what other kinds of knowledge would have to be used to bring about a more complete un-

46

derstanding of these same things. He must be faced with situations and asked to explain them by means of all the knowledge that he has—knowledge coming from his own experience, from his discussions, from his reading, etc. He must get into the habit of using his knowledge, all of it, as an ever-ready instrument for understanding what is met. In so doing he will develop a facility to see the relevance of the knowledge being acquired to both his former knowledge and the situations he has met and is meeting now.

Some sessions of the formal dialogue will consist in a common study of a particular situation by students and teachers. It will be a situation new to the teachers as well as to the students. The study will consequently be honest, and not merely a show staged by the teachers.

This diagnostic procedure of focusing knowledge on situations in order to explain them must accompany all learning as an integral part of it. Always, in every step of his coming to know, the student must be kept aware that the completion of his knowing lies in understanding things, and aware also of what gaps in his knowledge keep him from understanding these as well as he might. As he increases in knowledge he must make equal progress in knowing how to focus that knowledge.

Years ago I was driving through a Rocky Mountain valley in the dead of winter. The narrow road led through swampy country, then frozen over, and on each side of the road, elevating it a little from the swamp, was a low cribbing of logs. The car skidded on the ice and the rear wheels went over the log on the right side. This log was somewhat decayed, and the chains on the wheels gnawed deeply into the wood instead of lifting the car back onto the road. My companion was a thoroughly refined and educated gentleman. He got out of the car to look the situation over; and after mature deliberation he gave me the following advice: "Why don't you put the chains on the front wheels? They don't seem to be spinning." It is things like this that infuriate the common man and convince him that his contempt for the intellectual is justified.

The gentleman made his imbecilic suggestion about the chains because he thoroughly misunderstood the causal relations in the situation he was studying. He did not know what caused what. But it is just the correct seeing of the causal elements in a situation or event, or in the state of a person or thing, that enables one to understand it. Moreover, each of the ways of knowing carries with it an appreciation of its particular kind of causality; and the focusing of every kind of knowledge on one particular situation in order to understand it will mean, along with other things, the employing of all the different kinds of cause-and-effect relationships that we know. If one of these kinds of cause is neglected, we run the risk of misunderstanding the whole thing. We fail to understand a martyr, for instance, if we have no appreciation of the causal power of the love of God. (The Freudian explanation of the martyr is pitiful in its inadequacy. Whatever the martyr may have, one thing that he does not have is a martyr complex, although there are plenty of non-martyrs who do.)

What I mean by understanding a situation by means of a complete knowledge of its causes can be illustrated by the understanding a woodsman has of what goes on in the forest.

You can find here an intellectual activity of a high order, and you often find it among quite primitive people. You come to appreciate it and partially understand it, however, only when it is exercised by a quite unprimitive person who can explain it in terms intelligible to you, a person such as Jim Corbett, the hunter of man-eating tigers.

In his account of his work you see a wonderfully complex causal knowledge applied for the understanding of a particular situation. Everything that he sees, feels, smells, hears or is intuitively aware of indicates to him what is happening in the jungle beyond his range of vision. He knows what causes each of these phenomena. He infers, from what other animals are doing, what the tiger is doing; he predicts from the lay of the land, the direction of the wind, the time of day, and his own actions what the tiger, who is also hunting *him*, will do. Although he may never see the tiger until the time comes for the one and only shot, he knows during the long hunt where the tiger is and what he is doing, and he so arranges things that he and the tiger will meet at a certain time and in a place where the one shot will be possible.

There is no better example than this of the understanding of a complex situation by means of an exhaustive knowledge of all the cause-and-effect relationships that can apply. Something analogous to this, but on a level of much more complex causal relationships, is the knowledge, and the ability to focus it, that our intellectuals must have if they are to complete their knowing by understanding the world they live in. A man who is properly educated should possess this understanding to a high degree. He should be able to size up a situation by seeing how it got that way (that is, by knowing its causes) and by knowing what will happen as a result of it (that is, by knowing its effects).

Therefore, if higher education is to be adequate it must include some process effective in bringing about this causal knowledge, or rather, in arousing in the student a sharp awareness of the causal realities in all the knowledge that he has. Then he will become accustomed to think causally, and see every situation and every event not only in terms of what it is, but in terms of how it came to be and what will result from it.

The basic element in this attempt to understand in terms of cause and effect must be an appreciation of the manifoldness of the causal relation. Beatrice is one cause of Dante's literary excellence, but not in the same way that a lowering of the temperature is the cause of Walden Pond's freezing over. My counting the number of people in the room is the cause of the fact that I know their number. If I had not counted them I would not have known how many there were. But this kind of causal relation is quite different from that by which the bat sends the ball over the fence. When I say that an insult makes me angry, the word *makes* does not denote the same relation as it does when I say that clothes make the man. And the same word has still another denotation when I say that God made the world. Similarly, when I say that I got up early this morning in order that I might work in my garden, I do not mean the same thing by this *in order that* as I mean when I say that in order that there may be thought there must be a mind to think it.

Each one of these statements is the assertion of a causal relationship, yet no two of these relationships are of the same kind. And of course there are many more. The student must be made aware that just as there are many ways of knowing, so there are many ways in which one thing can be the cause or the effect of another, and that all the ways of knowing and all the kinds of causal relationship must be used in proper proportion if things are to be understood. He must be shown the unsatisfactory narrowness and unwisdom that lies in the attempt to explain things in just one causal way, such as the attempt to describe all that happens in the universe in terms of matter and motion, or the attempt to account for all human motives on the basis of the Freudian hypothesis, or the attempt to explain a movement in human history solely by economic determinism.

The teachers in the community must take care to prevent the narrowness that may come, in their own minds as well as in the minds of the students, through either an *a priori* rejection of a newly proposed kind of causal relation or an enthusiastic acceptance of it alone as a completely satisfactory explanation of a given situation. Some learned men would reject the Freudian hypothesis with dismay, and some with the ridicule of the Vienna wit who defined psychoanalysis as "that disease whose cure it claims to be." Many intelligent men have accepted it as the sole and sufficient explanation of everything that human beings do. Neither of these reactions is the way of the wise man. Our knowledge of the depths of the human personality has been enormously increased by Freudian psychology. It has given a new dimension to our thinking. But it can by no means give us all there is to know about why humans behave as they do.

The analysis of situations holds the place in understanding that the solution of problems holds in theoretical knowing. Therefore in a complete scheme of higher education such analysis plays an important part, and opportunity must be prepared for it by careful planning, with time for its learning.

There is a children's game that used to be called "Jack Straws." A person held up a handful of thin sticks about six inches long, and dropped them so that they fell in a haphazard pile. The game was to take a small hook and remove the sticks one by one from the pile in such a way that as each stick was removed, no other stick in the pile would move even slightly. The ability to do this requires a careful causal analysis of the situation. I have to examine the pile to discover the physical relation of each stick to every other. I have to know something of leverage and balance, and what the other end of a stick will do if I move one end with the hook. I have to forsee the consequences of every move I may make. As a result of this analysis I come to see that if I move this one particular stick in this one particular way the other sticks will not move at all. When this stick is successfully moved away the situation in the pile is altered and needs further study before I make the next move. And so until the pile is gone.

The same kind of analysis is made on a grander scale in the study of a log jam in a river, to find the key log whose dynamiting will break the jam and get the logs moving again. The person who would break the jam must study the relationships of stress and strain that exist between the logs in their various positions and must be able to foresee what will happen to each one of them if he dynamites any particular log.

We can teach the student what causal analysis means by facing him with simple situations in which the causal relations are all on the physical level, and can thus accustom him to viewing situations causally. Then the situations can be made more complicated, involving different kinds of knowing and the different kinds of causality that they imply, so that the student may habituate himself to look at all situations causally.

Let us imagine a situation which at first sight appears to be governed by purely physical causal relations, but which turns out to be far more complex.

On the hillside there is an oak tree which the owner wants cut down. We take the students to the spot to look over the situation. The tree is surrounded by other trees of various kinds and at different stages of growth. Let us make the preliminary causal analysis. If the tree is cut down it is going to fall. Since it is oak it is very heavy and can destroy what it crashes against. The student must look all around the tree, and must figure out what will happen if it falls in any possible direction. If it falls one way it will tear the big branch from a smaller oak. If it falls nearer the second oak it will crash against it and will not come to the ground at all, and the second oak will have to be felled in order to bring the first one down. If it falls in another direction it will crush some saplings that will be needed to fill the space left vacant by its removal. If it falls straight down the hill it will land in a rocky gully where it will be hard to saw it up into logs and harder still to get the logs out. Taking all those things into consideration, the students must determine the best direction for the tree to fall.

But then there must come another causal analysis, still on the physical plane. Considering all the elements in the situation, how are we to get the tree to fall in the direction we have chosen? Its angle of growth over the hillside and its general configuration being what they are, where is its center of gravity in relation to its base of support? If we should cut the trunk straight through at its base where would it fall "naturally"? How much could a slanting cut change its fall in the desired direction? How will the wind that is now blowing affect the direction of the fall? If we need the help of a rope, where in the tree should we tie it, and in what direction shall we pull in order that this pull will combine with all the other causal elements in the situation to make the tree fall exactly where we want it to?

Now we come to the human causal plane. Does the man who is operating the saw know what may happen when the tree begins to fall? Is he nimble enough to get out of the way, and is there space enough for him to get out of the way, if the trunk in falling takes an unexpected twist? Can he use an axe without taking a toe off? How long a rope must we use so that the tree, when it falls, will not fall on the men at the end of the rope?

There is still the esthetic level of cause and effect to be considered, and after that the moral level. What will the hillside look like with our tree removed and with the other destruction that will be caused by its fall? If the beauty of the place will be spoiled, should we be the agents of its spoiling? If we are free and responsible beings should we say to the owner (and here we are definitely on the moral level of causality), "Sorry, but we are convinced that the tree ought not to come down, for it will destroy the beauty of this hillside. We will not be the ones to bring about such a disaster. We urge you to reconsider."

By introducing the students to such comparatively simple causal situations and calling their attention to the many casual relations present even here, they will become accustomed to looking for the unobvious causes and effects in what they meet, and will form the habit of detecting the causal network that envelops existential reality everywhere.

This seeing of the causal network is particularly important for a person who is to influence other persons, for the one who is to be a leader. The student must be led to watch his own words and actions, be aware of what causes them and what effects they will have on other people. This assertion that I am about to make—do I make it because I believe it true, or because I am angry or jealous, or eager to make an impression? And the man to whom I say it—will he accept it, or be insulted and fight back, or will he simply yawn? In pure theory the validity of the reasoning may be all that counts, but in actual discussion it is not only the logic of what is said that counts, but also the way it is said, the motive behind it, and the situation of the man that hears it, so that if a person is to be truly understanding he must take all these elements into account.

In our insistence on the necessity of facing the student with situations which he must learn to understand by bringing all knowledge to bear and by finding out all the causal relationships involved, we have given several hypothetical examples. That is all that can be done in a book. But in teaching, hypothetical examples will not do. The student must be placed in real situations, and must make real decisions in regard to them. And these situations must be of the most varied kinds: simple and complex, physical, psychological, social, financial, religious, and moral.

It must be the planned practice of the community of understanding to take advantage of situations that arise naturally and to create situations where they do not arise naturally. Since one of the great failures of our educated men is their inability to understand less educated men, our students *must not* be allowed to fail here. If an education draws a man away from his family and neighbors, if it fosters an attitude of contempt or condescension for them, that man becomes less understanding all the time. His education has failed. He has grown not wise but foolish. If he were growing wise, he would grow in sympathy and understanding for all men, uneducated as well as educated.

A man who has been educated in understanding should be able to converse with an ignorant man and profit from the encounter.

There is an excuse for the uneducated man who fails to understand the man who has been to college. There is no excuse for the college man's failure to understand his uneducated brother—or father or mother. Yet how many times do we see the professed intellectual uncomprehending or bored when he finds himself outside his sophisticated circle?

Uneducated men will therefore be invited to the community of learning so that students and teachers will get to know them. They will be treated with the same respect that would be given to scholars, and their opinions given the same consideration. Every opportunity will be given the students to learn to appreciate the kind of excellence that can reside in the unacademic intellect, and the unsophisticated goodness that can be found in very simple people. The person who is altogether outside the academic tradition will often approach a problem with an originality which brings completely new insights, insights which the students should appreciate and learn to combine with the tradition that they are coming to know. The contact between the students and an uneducated man with a good mind can be most profitable for the intellectual training of the student.

Since the understanding of one's fellow human beings is one of the most important objects of education, the community must devote much of its attention to it. There will be the theoretical, scientific study of man. There will be the study of man through literature. There will be, as we have said, the association with widely different kinds of men. And there will be an acquaintance with some fundamental human situations which can only come through experience.

Knowledge by acquaintance is the only way in which some very important things can be understood, and therefore this way has an authentic place in an institution of higher learning. There are two fundamental human experiences which can be genuinely understood only in this way, and if they are not understood men are not understood. They are *work* and *play*. The opportunity to experience them must be included among the community's activities. Work will be considered not as a means of earning one's way, although it can very well be that, but as a way that leads the student to appreciate what he did not appreciate before and could not appreciate otherwise. And play will be considered not simply as a means of relaxation and refreshment, which it is, but as an activity which can lead to an appreciation of persons and things attainable in no other way.

In the physical toil involved in keeping the human race going, in hard labor in the hot sun or dogged perseverance in the bitter cold, in the blessedness of rest after toil and the warmth after cold, a person relives in himself much of the experience of most of the human race. If he does not know what it means to be bone tired and to have to keep going when he can barely stagger, and what rest means for the weary (for there is no true rest that is not preceded by toil), and if he has not experienced the joy that comes with the alternation of labor and rest, he is out of touch with his fellow men both past and present. He does not understand the human condition. He is not well educated.

Then there is the work that is the making of something, and the joy of accomplishment that comes with its success. If a person does not know what it is to conceive of something that he wants to make, to select the material, to fashion the material according to his conception and to modify the conception as he goes along according to the limitations that he finds in the material and the defects that show up in the conception itself, and then to view with satisfaction and sometimes with surprise what he has made, he has no appreciation of what it means to be a craftsman or an artist. There are important aspects of the human condition that are closed to him. He also is not well educated.

Work, then, is an experience which helps a person understand his fellow men. It is one of the means of liberal education. But its educative value is not confined to helping one understand human beings. It is also a means of understanding other things in the world, living and non-living. The world of human artifice that so overwhelmingly surrounds most people throughout their lives shuts them out almost completely from an understanding of the world apart from man, and yet an understanding of this world as it really is is an integral part of the totality of knowing. If a person has not understood animals and plants he is ignorant with a vast ignorance, and he can be thus ignorant even when he knows biology. Working with plants and animals, and playing with them, brings about an acquaintance that is the opposite of ignorance.

"The innate cussedness of inanimate objects" has bewildered intellectuals ever since there have been intellectuals. Even though they have known physics they have looked on with helpless dismay when the hammer struck the thumb, when the moist hand froze to the door knob, when the other end of the ten-foot board wrought destruction while they were steering one end of it through the dining room, or when the boat in which one foot was planted so quickly slid away from the dock where the other foot had set itself. But a little time spent in working with tools on different things in different places in different seasons would make the behavior of these inanimate objects seem less cussed and more predictable. A person can become at home with them, and can live rationally with them and by means of them. Since he has to live in a world of things as well as people, a misunderstanding of the behavior of things will be a disastrous ignorance.

Play is the complement of work, in knowing as well as in living. Just as after a period of planned, serious purposeful effort the human being needs a period in which he can act spontaneously or even whimsically or, if he wishes, not act at all, both periods forming a valuable part of his living, so also, along with hard work as a means of understanding people and things, there is a complementary understanding that comes from taking things lightly, from a haphazard, unplanned wandering with them and among them, or from simply existing among them in a *dolce far niente*. Who would think that one could understand a dog without playing with him? Or a man? And a recent book has shown us that lions can be understood that way too.

It is in times of play that many insights come. Of all human activities play is most like contemplation, and play in which no other human beings are involved can scarcely be distinguished from it.

This brings us to perhaps the most significant of the situations in which understanding can be gained: contemplation in solitude. We have already said that the true life of learning will consist in alternate entry into the dialogue and withdrawal from it. The withdrawal is not anti-social. It is a necessary part of community lift, for from it comes enrichment of the whole community, for the dialogue itself as well as for the member who temporarily withdraws.

The most obvious thing that is done in the time of withdrawal is private study and investigation. The other thing that should happen is contemplation.

There is a story of an old man who spent most of his time sitting on his front porch, his chair tipped back against the house wall. When someone asked him what he did all that time he replied, "Sometimes I set and think, and sometimes I just set." "Setting and thinking" would perhaps be meditation, the purposeful effort to figure things out; and "just setting" could be contemplation, the effortless opening of the mind to whatever comes. Both of these practices are valuable uses of solitude. They are valuable in theoretical knowing, in coming to know the relation of ideas to one another. They are also valuable in coming to understand particular persons, things, events and situations.

Figuring things out in solitude is universally recognized as a way of coming to know; but contemplation is not so highly valued in our world, where accomplishment is measured by the amount of buzzing around one does. And yet the practice of simply allowing the mind to remain open to what comes, with no straining toward knowing and no effort to fill the openness with anything, is a way in which great understanding comes. In this attitude of pure receptiveness things happen to a person. The elements of a situation he has been studying fall into place so that he finally understands. A sudden appreciation of a person he has been thinking about flashes on his mind. He becomes aware all at once that he understands the motive behind an action that has been puzzling him. There is no more valuable way of coming to know and understand than the way of contemplation, and this way must be provided for in the community.

If we seem to have been unduly long in our description of the community of understanding it is because we are here dealing with an aspect of true higher education that is not usually recognized, and when recognized will perhaps be denied with vigor. But we must insist that the people who go through our existing process of higher education show a great deficiency precisely where such people should not be deficient. They lack wisdom and they lack the ability to lead. And this deficiency is not there in spite of the education they have received but because of it, for this education has not led them to a breadth of knowing, and it has not led them to focus their knowledge for the purpose of understanding existential situations.

If, in the process of learning to know, the student is not also learning *to understand*, he is learning *not to understand*. He is being mis-educated.

* * *

6

It will be obvious that in the kind of scholastic community we have been describing the method of estimating the status and evaluating the attainments of students will have to be quite different from what it is in the conventional college. Our college is above all a human institution; and in this matter of evaluation we must, in order to keep it human, fight the great American lust for system and statistics. There is very much in the student's life of learning that had better be left to his own organizing rather than to ours; and there is much in it also that we do not need to know, and in this case our desire to find out becomes a mere snooping. There is no need to take a person's temperature every day and keep a record of it.

An educational institution has a right to make public declaration that a certain student has, in the opinion of its authorities, become what these authorities have wished him to become. It has the right to put the stamp of approval upon him. It also has the right to put the stamp of disapproval on another of its students. In order thus to approve or disapprove, the institution must provide some means of ascertaining where a student stands. There must be examination in some form, but examination really suited to what examination can and should accomplish.

There are three distinct functions that an examination can perform: to determine whether or not a student is to be admitted into the community, to determine his progress in becoming what the community wants him to become, and to determine his final standing. These three kinds of examination are quite distinct one from the other. Their results must never be confused with one another, nor may the result of one be rightly used to influence the result of another.

The purpose of the entrance examination will be to find out whether the prospective student really wants to learn, whether he is capable of doing so, and whether he is willing and able to take part in the life of the community of learning and understanding. There must therefore be some means of weeding out the unwilling, the stupid and the unbalanced. For this initial sifting the standard tests and letters of recommendation can be used, and it is doubtful if these tests and letters will have any further value for us. The candidates who survive this first process of selection will have to be examined by the college itself, not by a testing service. They will have to be given a searching interview, and will have to explain in writing why they want to come to the college, what they are willing to give up in order to learn, and what their future plans are.

The playboy and the man who comes to college because of parental or other social pressure will be refused admission no matter how high an ability a test shows him to have. The extent of previous schooling will not be considered, nor will the age of the applicant. A school whose standards of admission would keep out an Abraham Lincoln is a school whose standards of admission are false. The person of average or above average intelligence who really wants to learn and is willing to make sacrifices in order to learn is the student needed.

If it were possible to pick out potential leaders, such persons would be the ones to have priority in admission to our school, for since they are going to determine to a large extent the opinions and actions of their neighbors and hence of their communities, it would be well for all of us that they learn to determine wisely. Even though there seems to be no sure way to find out whether a given young person is going to be such a leader, we should recognize potential leadership as a quality much to be desired in a student in our college. If this college and others like it could find and educate these men who will lead society from within, our country could safely leave the high offices of government to men from schools of the more traditional kind.

After the entrance examination we may examine a student to find out what progress he is making in knowing and understanding. The legitimate purpose of such a testing would be to enable both teacher and student to know how the student is progressing, what special attention should be paid in the immediate future to certain phases of his training, whether he should be allowed to take the next step in the school's program, or whether he should be asked to leave. But this kind of examination would be purely private. It would help to guide both student and teacher in their future relations with each other. Once done it would have served its purpose and should be forgotten, surviving only in the actions of student and teacher. The result should not be allowed to remain to form a statistic.

The third purpose of examination is to make possible a final evaluation of the student when he is about to leave the community and wishes to have the community's stamp of approval upon him. This examination will allow the teachers to know whether this stamp of approval should be given, and will also enable them, if they wish to do so, to place the student in relation to the other students who are graduating, in an order of excellence.

These three kinds of examination differ essentially from one another in their character and in the use that can legitimately be made of them. The entrance examination commits us to taking or rejecting the student. If we take him, he is a member of the community. The examination has served its purpose. Its papers should be quietly burned so that it will not survive to haunt anyone. No one should remember it in any way in dealing with the student.

The second kind of examination, which can be rare or frequent, according to the wish of the individual teacher, is an instrument of expediency to be used and thrown away. The papers should be burned, the ashes scattered to the winds. It is a way of discovering what to do next. Once we have decided, its further remembrance can do only harm. The third kind of examination has a finality about it. It is a matter of permanent record, there forever for all to see. It must be the only examination that matters.

One of the great confusions of means and ends that we find in our conventional colleges is the common practice with regard to examinations and the uses made of them. The results of examinations given along the way, which should be used purely for our guidance, are preserved, and from them is computed (quite literally computed on a machine) the final evaluation of the student. And a final examination, which might be of value in showing what has happened to a person's mind during his years in college, is not given at all.

This is in effect what we do. We say that at a certain time student John Brown answered certain questions on American history in a satisfactory way. At another time he answered some questions about English literature. On another day he solved some problems in algebra; on another he wrote an acceptable essay. Since he has done these prescribed things we consider him worthy of our degree. And we use the results of all these along-the-way testings to compute an *average,* which places John Brown in relation to the others on the list of graduates. But we make no effort at the end of his college career to find out what he knows, to see if he remembers what he has learned, whether it has become a part of an integral and usable thought-world, whether he is able to think and write and read intelligently, and to focus his knowledge and skill. The one thing that is really worthwhile — what his entire education at our school has amounted to—we make no effort to learn. We give all the examinations except the one which would have permanent value.

In a vast accumulation of not too effective academic customs, the "average" is perhaps the most useless. Let us consider a case, exaggerated so as to be more easily seen. Suppose a young man comes to our college and at first does excellent work that we would rate at 100. And suppose that by the end of his four years with us he is doing work that we rate at 40. His average will be 70. Then suppose another young man whose work at the beginning rates 40 and at the end 100. His average will also be 70. Here are two men, one whose academic career has been a complete failure and the other whose career is an astounding success, yet they have the same average and their rank among their fellow students will be the same. The average shows nothing worth knowing because it does not show direction. It prevents both good students and bad students from getting proper guidance and recognition.

How will the process of examination go on in our community of learning? It will be obvious that since there is no uniform and prescribed *cursus honorum* that the students will have to go through in order to graduate they cannot be evaluated on their specific accomplishments as they progress. This means that grades and credits for courses will not be given because courses in the usual meaning of the term will not exist. Since so much of what the students learn will be learned in the formal and informal dialogues, and since each person's participation in these dialogues will be unique, there will be no standard stages at which they can be graded even if one desired to do so. Since the students will be learning so many things in so many ways, none of these ways will be considered sufficiently "official" to "count" while other ways do not count. They all count, and the only way to evaluate a student in a regime where all knowledge and all ways of knowing count is to examine him solely on what he knows and how he can use his knowledge when he comes to the end of his time in our college.

This examination, designed to find out what the student knows and does not know and to measure his ability to use that knowledge and the skills he has acquired in the process of mastering it, must be one which evaluates what he has gained by all the means of education that he has used. It must therefore be a distinct process rather than an appendage to one particular process of learning, and it must come as the final step of the student's career at the college.

An examination which is to determine a school's evaluation of one of its students is of critical importance to the school and to the student. It may determine the standing of the student, but it also determines the honesty of the school. It must be a prolonged, straightforward and sincere effort on the part of the examiners to determine where the student stands. Consequently it must be an altogether different thing from what examinations usually are. No standardized testing service could possibly give it. It cannot be so constituted as to save the examiners' time.

I am not particularly disturbed by the increase (if it exists) of cheating in examinations. It is immoral, yes; but it is a return in kind for the immoral examinations set by the teachers. The examination is immoral in placing an evaluation, and a public one at that, on the intellectual accomplishment of the student by means totally inadequate for assessing his intellectual accomplishment. The student in turn cheats by using unlawful ways of turning these essentially inadequate means to his own advantage. Suppose you are giving a history course. At the end of it you give an examination. There will be many papers to correct. The reading of each one must not take too long. So you ask ten questions. You assume that if the students have learned anything in the course they will know the answers to most of these questions. Of course this is not true at all. Such is the intricacy of the human mind, its mysterious insights and its equally mysterious lacunae, its tricks of remembering and forgetting, that the student could quite well know much of what was dealt with in the course and still not be able to answer these questions. He might be able to answer these questions satisfactorily and know little more. You, the teacher, are giving the student a public status, good or bad, which you determine by means that are inadequate and therefore unjust: his answering or failing to answer ten questions. The student, in return, seeks to have his standing assured by means equally unjust: learning the correct answers to the questions from the better student sitting beside him. The giving of the questions and the answering of them are on the same low moral level.

But there is not enough time! It is absolutely impossible, you say, to make an honest and adequate evaluation of each student in the time available. If this is really the case the answer is obvious: We should not make any public evaluation. Such a statement, which gives the student a status important to him and which is taken very seriously by society at large, can rightly be made only if it can be made with complete honesty. And in a situation so serious for the student, a situation by which to some extent his future is determined, we must be willing to take the time that justice requires. Wherever we cut corners to save time it must not be here. We must examine either adequately or not at all.

The argument from lack of time is a good argument against giving examinations at frequent intervals in order to determine an average; but the fact that averages mean nothing significant is another and stronger reason for not giving them. The preliminary tests that *are* permissible, those given merely to enable the teacher to know how to deal with the student in the future, can be given (though they are admittedly inadequate), because they play no part in determining the student's standing before the world.

But what of the examination that does determine the student's standing, the one designed to find out what his intellectual situation really is as a result of his years at college? How can it be made adequate?

It cannot be short, and it cannot be mechanical. It is a matter of honestly trying to find out what another person knows, thinks, and is able to do in a certain field of human life. Therefore the examination has to be devised with great care, prepared by people who know the one to be examined. For example, a test which might well give a fluent person opportunity to show what he knows could be a complete failure if given to a man who finds articulation difficult. (Our usual practice is to assign to the student the failure that really belongs to the examiner.)

An adequate examination must be suited to the character of the person to be examined. It must be thorough. It must examine the student's strengths and weaknesses in all areas of knowing and understanding. What is his appreciation of the different ways of knowing? How does he express himself orally and in writing, and does he really have much to say? How well can he read and understand a difficult expository book, or a work of fiction? How well can he concentrate on an arduous problem and give us a solution? Is he willing to listen to others and try to understand them? How far has he been able to organize all his knowledge and skill in understanding, in order to begin to know God, the world, men and human society? How far is he aware of his own limitations and the reasons for them? Does he show interest in knowing more and understanding better? Is he able to use solitude as a means of knowing? Can he learn and teach in the dialogue?

To discover this and more the examiners will have to place themselves and the student in many situations, and the skill of the examiners will show in the situations they are able to devise for effective testing. To test a man adequately in this manner requires time, care, and ingenuity. It requires also a procedure that is completely different from what goes on in a conventional college.

We must first take drastic action in the matter of time. The last few months—the last semester if we follow the semester plan —of the student's time in college will be devoted to the final examination. We can call it the semester of evaluation. During this time we will see that the student is placed in all the situations we have devised to find out what we want to know about him. And we will have to devise enough situations so that his particular talents and weak points will be revealed. We will talk to him privately. We will give him periods of formal oral examination in different subjects. We will expose him to discussion with his classmates. We will have him explain a difficult problem to underclassmen. We will put him alone with a difficult book for a week, and see how he has understood it. We will put him alone with his thoughts for a week and see what has happened to him. He will be placed where he will have to use his knowledge for unravelling a complicated situation, for explaining how it came to be and what will result from it. He will be given assignments in different kinds of writing—expository, investigatory, descriptive, imaginative, and evaluative.

In an examination of this kind a person will have ample opportunity to show what he knows well and can do well, and to show what he knows but poorly and what he cannot do well. The strong and the weak sides of his intellectual life will be revealed to the examiners and to himself. And he will know that the standing given him is the result of honest testing.

When an extended examination such as this is proposed it will of course be maintained that the time required for it cannot possibly be taken from the total time of education, for the time allotted to learning would then be curtailed to an impossible degree.

This contention is true if we make a distinction between learning and being examined (and the distinction is valid if by examination we mean the conventional examination). But an examination such as we have suggested is not something separate from learning. It would be the culmination of the learning process in the college, and the student could well find that he had learned more, that he had acquired a greater integration and appreciation of what he had learned, and that he had received more new insights during this period of extended examination than during the whole of his previous time in college. If he has come to college because he wants to know—and there is no other valid reason for coming at all—this final period will be the period of greatest joy for him, because in it he will come to realize what he knows and does not know. And the examination itself, not just the preparation for the various parts of it, will give him more enlightenment as he goes through it, so that he will come to know, right then, much that he did not know before. A good examination is an effective way of teaching as well as of testing.

A word now about high standards. When we hear the expression "raising our standards" we ordinarily think of adopting a system of techniques for weeding out less intelligent students and forcing the more intelligent students to work harder. But this attitude is on a rather low intellectual level. Threatening people, kicking them in the pants to make them move, worrying about what Harvard will think of us or how the Phi Beta Kappa committee will view us, hiring distinguished professors to impress the academic world—this temper of mind has nothing to do with intellectual eminence. Where such considerations reign, genuinely high standards become almost impossible.

What then are really "high standards"? High standards exist in an educational institution when what happens there helps, develops, inspires and satisfies the very best of the students, so that no one of them can honestly say that his intellectual life has been cramped or frustrated by his membership in the community. This situation is created and maintained when teachers and students would all of them gladly learn and gladly teach. When those in authority in the college become policemen or public relations men and are concerned with the image of the school in the mind of the public, the situation is disrupted. One is justified in saying that in the truly great educational institutions in our tradition, we have not been too concerned lest a few lazy or ignorant students get into the school and stay in. Their greatness has consisted in what was going on within. Their intellectual level has been maintained by attraction rather than by exclusion. And the attraction of a genuine intellectual life can transform the lazy and the ignorant into men zealous to know because they have come to love knowing.

Our proposed community of learning, therefore, will attain and maintain its standards rather by the reality of its intellectual life than by the fierceness of its requirements. It will truly be a free city of the mind.

* * *

7

The Ph.D. degree has probably been the object of more ridicule than any other gadget in the academic bag of tricks. It has been laughed at not only by the general public but by the very educators who so strenuously seek it and rigorously demand it of those whom they are going to employ to teach. And I will say that the degree eminently justifies all the ridicule that it has received. Its requirements for academic advancement shows how far from reality college administrators have come.

But the phrase in its original meaning is holy: Doctor of Philosophy, *teacher of the love of wisdom*. And a person in the teaching profession who has acquired that degree in his youth, acquired it perhaps only as a union card to get into the profession, can well spend the rest of his life trying to live up to its real meaning, even though in the attempt he finds it more and more necessary to disregard the existing rules and standards of the profession which has forgotten the meaning and the holiness of the words engraved on the card.

Teacher of the love of wisdom—not teacher of wisdom, for who could do that?—but a teacher who tries to lead his students to catch sight of the beauty of wisdom, to love it and seek it! This is the person who will be the teacher in our community of learning and understanding; and we will restore to a debased title its former dignity and call our teacher Doctor of Philosophy, whether or not he happens to have the degree. Just as the college we have been describing differs from conventional colleges and universities and must consequently employ a different method of evaluating its students, so also must it seek the services of a different kind of teacher. It goes without saying that this teacher must have knowledge, but he must also have a love of wisdom, be himself seeking it, and recognize a vocation to lead other people to it.

This new kind of teacher will be quite unlike the conventional college teacher. Since the training a man receives in order to be allowed to teach in a conventional school is likely to unfit him for becoming a true doctor of philosophy, such training will not be required at our school. Indeed, if our prospective teacher does have the Ph.D. degree, we will have to be assured that the obtaining of it has not ruined his love of wisdom and his desire and ability to lead others to that love; for the training he has received may have so confirmed him in some specialized way of thinking that he is unable and unwilling to recognize the claims of any other.

The doctor of philosophy's love of wisdom must be the antithesis of that spirit of specialization which drives a person to follow one path of knowing alone, disregarding all others. Although he will inevitably be more interested in some ways of knowing than in others, he must have a respect for all, and a willingess to grant a place of dignity to all knowledge. He must have an insatiable desire to know more, and stretch the limits of his own comprehension. But this constant extension of his own knowledge need not be aimed at an increase in the world's knowledge. There will be no insistence on "original contributions" and certainly no demand that he should publish anything. Our teacher will learn in order that he may know more and be a better teacher, not in order that our college may become famous.

The true teacher, having an essential respect for all knowledge, will be most careful not to dismiss a theory, an idea, a moral estimate or an assertion of fact until he has made an adequate investigation by which he can distinguish the good and the true in it from the evil and the false. It is only with this kind of respect that he can enter into the dialogue which will be such an essential part of his work at the college.

He must also have a deep respect for what there is to be known, that is, to use the philosophical term, for *being*. He must be interested in what is and in what happens, and must have an appreciation of metaphysical knowing, the effort of the human mind to understand the fundamental "kinds" of reality and their relations to each other, so that the things that we know can be put in their proper places in the system of what is, so that we can

70

escape the solipsism and the relativism that block many ways to inquiry.

The doctor of philosophy is not only a lover of wisdom; he is a teacher, and that means that besides wisdom he must love the student whom he is trying to lead to the love of wisdom. This love will consist not so much in affection as in a devotion to the student's intellectual and moral welfare, an understanding of his problems, a reverence for him as a person and for his intellectual efforts and positions even when they are weak, a willingness to use severity as a pedagogical device when necessary, and an endless patience. His love must also extend to the community so that he will be concerned for its success, participate in its life and bring to it the results of his own intellectual effort.

I realize that partisans of the German *Fachmann* mentality will object to our teacher as "amateur" and "dilettante." But the teacher can accept with thanks and with enthusiasm these words intended as slander, for both of them are derived from words meaning *love*. The connotation of lack of seriousness has been intruded into their meaning by scholars, members of a trade not known for love—and intruded falsely, for love cannot but be serious.

The teacher in our community of learning has the task and the privilege of associating with a person who wants to know and understand, in such a way that this person will be assisted and guided in his efforts and inspired to still greater efforts. As a doctor of philosophy the teacher is responsible for the person and mind of the student rather than for the "subject" that is being taught, for it is love of wisdom that he is trying to engender. He must therefore study the student in order to know how and in what order subjects are to be presented to him to lead him to the love of wisdom.

Let us look at the teacher-learner situation as it concerns the teacher and the young person who is of an age to realize the value of coming to know.

Facing this student there is the *world*, by which I mean the sum-total of what is, in all its variety. This the student wants to know and understand as far as he is able. When he comes to college he meets, in a form much more complete than he has ever

71

met it before, the *tradition,* that great body of knowledge, skills, evaluations and aspirations that the human race has constructed in its thinking about the world and about itself. This tradition is not simply a museum of ancient lore. It is a repository of recorded human thought from the remotest antiquity up to last night. Our institutions of higher learning are at least supposed to be the custodians of this tradition.

The teacher is presumed to be a person who has already come to know something of the world and of the tradition. His job is to introduce the student to the tradition, and through it to the world in such a way that the student's knowledge of the world will be developed and corrected by it, and that the student himself may in the process become a man of larger comprehension and more precise discrimination. But a part of this learning process must be an accompanying criticism whereby the student learns to correct the tradition by a direct investigation of the world and by his own thinking. He should come to regard the tradition as a glorious instrument of knowing and understanding, not as a final authority; and he should come to think of its great men as revered friends rather than as masters. Most of all, he should be so taught that his present human teacher does not become his master. Truth is the master, and human teachers can miss the truth.

Now to come down to actualities. Assuming that our community of learning is in operation, that our doctor of philosophy is a member of it, and that our student has been accepted as a new member, what is it, exactly, that is to happen?

The teacher is at the beginning made responsible for a general supervision of the student during a certain part of his time in the community. He is to lead him to the love of wisdom. He is to do this in the way that seems best *for that particular student.* But before he knows the student well enough to be able to know what way to lead him, there are certain things he will always do. He will lead the student to the formal dialogue and introduce him to the members of the community and get him started in the community life, perhaps assigning some older students to look out for him. Then he will start him on his career of personal study— reading and writing on assigned topics, attending lectures, and joining groups making particular investigations. As he gets to

72

know the student better he will modify the program, in consultation with the student himself, so that the student can use to best advantage whatever is going on in the community.

As time goes on the teacher's supervision will diminish and the student will ultimately manage his own life of study, consulting with the teacher only when he wishes. The skill and the love of the teacher will be shown as much in his willingness to let the student travel his own road as in his willingness to assume the obligation of teaching him. Perhaps the end of his tuition will come in his leading the student to teach other students, for teaching others is one of the best ways of learning.

In the time when he is superintending the student's intellectual progress, the teacher must not so lose himself in the details of the work that he neglects his main job: leading him to the love of wisdom. The man who loves to read and think and talk about history must learn what mathematical thinking is, and what its methods are and what its value is. He will otherwise be doomed to the ignorance of the specialist. One's enthusiasm for physics must not be allowed to prevent his giving serious and respectful attention to the consideration of faith as a means of arriving at truth and understanding. And the doctor of philosophy must bring about this broadening of outlook without quenching the spark of interest in one particular subject with which the student already burns.

As the students and teachers go along together the particular needs of each student will begin to appear. No two of them can be treated the same way, nor can any two teachers, because of the differences in their characters, treat the same student in the same way. Each teacher has to discover the best way for *him* to handle situations. It is here, in the personal guidance of one man by another, that the teacher's unique art is needed. And this art cannot be effectively exercised if students are taught only in large groups. Large numbers of people can be taught in lectures, and the full membership of the community can meet together in the formal dialogue; but these large gatherings are complementary to personal tuition, not substitutes for it. The teacher will do his most valuable work in meetings with individual students.

The student who is really uninterested in coming to know will be excluded from our college by the entrance examination. There is absolutely nothing to attract him to such a school and the teacher in consequence will not have the hopeless task of trying to teach him.

But among students sincerely desiring to know there will be some who are slow, some diffident, some inarticulate, and some whose vocabulary far outruns their control. Each one is a problem for special handling by the teacher, and in our college each one can be handled separately.

It is with the genuinely able student, however, that the work of the teacher is most critical in its effect. Here a potentially wise man can be developed or spoiled. This man who can so easily outdistance the others can also easily be so overcome with boredom that he comes to hate the college and everyone in it. It is in dealing with this kind of man that what we have said about high standards has its meaning. A major effort must be made by the community not to fail such a student. We must try to lead him along the road to wisdom as far as we can go, and then inspire him to go on ahead, opening the way for the rest of us.

The teacher will have a very wide latitude in dealing with such a student because of the kind of teaching-learning situation provided by the community. The student does not have to be forced into any kind of regimentation. His teacher can plan for him a way totally different from that taken by any other student. He can go as fast and as far as he is willing and able, for he is not travelling in a convoy where all must wait for the slowest; and neither is he restricted by the limits of the teacher's knowledge, for the teacher will direct him to the tradition, which bears the thoughts of the greatest men, and beyond that to the world of reality which he can study directly so far as his own powers will allow. There is no reason why he should not outdistance the teacher, and no reason why the teacher, when outdistanced, cannot still be a help and an encouragement. The lack of rigidity in our college, where the categories of teacher and student do not constitute a two-caste system, will allow the student who has surpassed his teacher to become the teacher of his teacher and of the other students. In the dialogue, formal and informal, the accomplishments of one can bring about advancement in knowing for everyone.

When the teacher has the advantage of not standing in a position of official authority (as the title *professor* would imply) but rather has the position of doctor of philosophy, he does not have to uphold that authority against the student's threatened superiority. It is natural and normal that some students should have greater ability than some teachers, and as they become more skilled in using this ability, it is natural and normal that they should excel these teachers in many ways. Since it is one of the teacher's jobs to make intellectual potentiality actual, he should be glad when he succeeds and the student who *can* outdistance him actually *does* outdistance him. This rather painful rejoicing comes more easily when there is no academic status which proclaims the teacher an authority.

Even when outdistanced the doctor of philosophy still has a very definite duty of guidance. He must work to lead this student's accomplishments and his intellectual brilliance into true wisdom. Not only must he strive to keep the student from becoming merely a specialist, but he must do his best to prevent his yielding to the temptations which entice so many brilliant men into becoming intellectuals and nothing more. There is the temptation to arrogance, to contempt for and impatience with the less intelligent and the less educated. There is the temptation to find satisfaction in cleverness and originality, in the epigram and the witty jest. There is the temptation to rest in one's superiority and the praise of one's fellows.

The very fact of a student's superiority of intellect will make him difficult to guide, and yet guidance here is of the greatest importance; for the world is full of brilliant men, and so few of them are wise. If instead of arrogance there can come for the student an appreciation of excellence in a man who is not an intellectual, if there can come a realization of what it means to a man to be mediocre or stupid, and if there can come an awareness that he himself has his mediocrities and stupidities, then there can rise in this brilliant student a comprehension which grows in the direction of wisdom. If this student can come to see that cleverness and wit are valuable social accomplishments indeed, and not to be despised, but that they are not accomplishments to be rested in or depended on, and that one must go beyond them to a serious seeking after truth, then he is growing in wisdom. And if he can be led to establish for himself his own interior discipline which will lead him toward knowing and understanding after he has passed the range of approval of his fellows and of his teachers, that also points toward wisdom.

The doctor of philosophy has to see that these realizations take place in his brilliant students, and it will take all his skill, prudence, planning, and a lot of his praying. He has to know how to work to *make* these things happen, but he also has to know how and when to sit back and *let* things happen, and when to let someone else do what he himself cannot do as well. He has to do all this, moreover, without attracting the student to himself as to a master; for when students attach themselves to human masters the first things and sometimes the only things that they acquire are the master's idiosyncracies, and a cult-circle is formed whose outward mark is a way of combing the hair and whose chief inner characteristic is a contempt for the rest of the world.

One of the advantages of the teacher-learner relationship we propose is the fact that so much is learned by the student that is not intentionally taught by the teacher, and so much learned by the teacher, that there is no occasion for one to look to the other with sentiments of awed and worshipful gratitude. Gratitude can rightly be directed both ways when no one is master.

What position among men could be more blessed and truly great than the position of doctor of philosophy in a community of learning. For one possessed even of the vision of such a calling, all the petty worries of current academic life—rank, promotion, and even salaries—evaporate in irrelevance. A great tragedy of our higher learning is that there are many men able and longing to become true doctors of philosophy but there are no positions for them in the prevailing academic structure. But more of this in another place.

Every vocation is a calling to some kind of servitude, some kind of bondage freely undertaken, and the doctor of philosophy is bound to devote his life to teaching people to love wisdom: to inspire people to begin to love and to seek it, and with all his ability to help those who are seeking it. His first obligation, if he is teaching in a college, even a college ill suited to his calling, is to the students and other teachers in the institution, but there will always be outsiders who want to learn, and these also, insofar as he knows them and they know him, have a claim on him. Others—administrators, potential donors, and the great ones of the earth—can be turned away if necessary, but the man who really wants to know has a right to the teacher's time, not in proportion to his importance but in proportion to the earnestness of his wanting to know. He cannot be brushed off, and attention to him can be restricted only when others who want to know call for the teacher's attention.

The sincerity of those who say they want to know can be tested only if they are attended to respectfully. For the teacher to turn away a person with the least glimmering of desire for wisdom is to break the bruised reed and to quench the smouldering flax; it may be to destroy the spirit of a man. And the glimmer can only be detected on close examination. The teacher will have to sacrifice many things that are valuable to him: his convenience, his schedule, his recreation, his sleep, his health, his career. Like the physician, he is on call any time, and like the physician he must answer the call. Only demands of equal importance—to religion, to family or to society—can interfere.

The thing that is most difficult to sacrifice in our present situation is the scholarly career, for it is this career that would win for the teacher his recognition and advancement. Writing for learned journals, attending the meetings of professional societies, applying for funds to carry on research and acting in such a way that the funds will be granted, getting to know the right people—all this takes much time, and unless time is spent on these things the academic career languishes. Yet the doctor of philosophy, if he really is one, must put down the book, or turn away from the typewriter, when even the least interesting student knocks at his door.

This surrender of careerist activities in order to give time to students does not at all mean giving up the search for wisdom. The beauty of such a calling is that the very process of trying to teach the love of wisdom is a process of learning to love wisdom more. The teaching-learning relationship is always more profitable for the teacher than it is for the learner; for the teacher presumably has a larger body of experience and more practical skill, so that the least spark enkindled in a discussion can be more enlightening for him than for the student. There is a chance that something like this may take place every time a student knocks at the door. Is there any greater chance of it if the president of the institution should knock at the door?

But it is in his relationship with the really good students that the teacher's own learning gains its principal acceleration. They show the inconsistencies in one's thought that must be resolved. They force one's mind to stretch itself in unforseen directions, always shaming one into reading the book that has been put off for years. It is with this kind of student that, in the flexible system of our community of learning, the teacher can put himself in due season into the position of pupil without the loss of any official dignity.

This education of the teacher goes on in all directions. There is a constant deepening in the understanding of what is already known, and also an extension of knowing in many ways. There is a growing ability to understand people and to deal with them. There is an increasing capacity of measuring what comes along in terms of what one has already seen. And by thinking along with young people the dangers of having one's knowing and understanding coming to an end are negligible. The sparks of enlightenment that a person received in his twenties, in the period of formal higher education, are few compared to the illuminations that can come in his sixties, for there is now a solid back-log of forty years' learning for the sparks to enkindle. There is no reason why this acceleration should not go on as long as life lasts.

The medieval University of Paris showed great good sense in seeing that its masters of arts, the actual teachers, remained its ruling power even when it became a great center of technical scholarship and gathered to itself some of the most learned theologians, physicists, physicians and legists of Europe. The men who taught the liberal arts to undergraduates set the policy and made the laws for the university. Their representative, the Rector of the Faculty of Arts, was the head of the institution and held a position of great honor in the world. Thus the supreme dignity of the teacher was recognized.

As we have already said, in our community of learning there can well be specialist scholars in residence, living there because the atmosphere is congenial to them, and there can be artists in residence also. These will be a great addition to the life of the community, and their very presence will be a stimulus to teaching and learning. But their life and work will not be the center of things. No effort should be made to advance the prestige of the school by importing distinguished scholars and artists.

The administration of our community will be in the hands of those who are the center of its life—the teachers and the students. The teachers, who consitute the permanent core of the institution, will naturally have more administrative power than the students, but the students, once each has shown his willingness and his ability to join in the life of the school, will have an important share of power and responsibility. The teachers as a corporate body will constitute the legal community and will own whatever property the community possesses. They will receive new teachers and decide on the dismissal of those who are unsatisfactory. They will admit the students and decide their status.

There will be no board of trustees, no administration distinct from the teachers and students. The community of learning, if it is to do its work of education properly, must be autonomous. *It must be a free city.* This is absolutely essential. The work of the doctor of philosophy cannot possibly be carried on with full effectiveness if he is an employee, to be hired and fired by an administration. He must be a free agent, subject only to the community of his equals. It is only in a regime of freedom that the full potentiality of teaching and learning can be released.

* * *

8

We have sketched the structure and the processes of the free city of the mind. We have shown how the teaching-learning activity will be carried on there. Now it is time to say something about what will be taught and presumably learned there.

Two things are clear. First, we are educating a man to be a more perfect man, not to be a butcher or baker, banker or lawyer. If we can be said to be preparing him for the future, we are preparing him for it by giving him the greatest possible interior resources. It is ridiculous, of course, to prepare him for any particular future, for no one knows what is going to happen. The student we are now teaching may have to live in a world of computers and push-buttons, and he must be fitted to live as a wise, good and free man in that world. He may, on the other hand, find himself existing as one of the few survivors in a world disintegrated by nuclear war with, as the phrase goes, "civilization as we know it" destroyed. Our student must therefore be prepared to survive and live among the other survivors as a wise man, knowing what is worth rebuilding, and beginning to build it.

With these goals to be striven for it is obvious that in the few years the student spends with us there will not be enough time to load him with information. We want him to go out into the world with an effective instrument for understanding what he meets, rather than with full archives of knowledge. We are not trying to produce learned men. We are trying to produce thinking and understanding men, men who will be able to become learned in any field of scholarship they may choose, or competent in any practical field they may select.

The student will come to us already possessing much information, gained in his former schooling and in his other experience. He will gain more while he is with us. Our chief interest in it will be to lead him to organize it, to relate the elements in it to one another, to make him conscious of how he knows it and with what degree of certainty he holds it. We want him to build it into a thought-world whose constitution he is aware of, so that he will know the unity in it where such exists, and will also recognize and evaluate the inconsistencies that are there: the unresolved difficulties of positions that cannot yet be reconciled but are nevertheless accepted, and the confident assurances that cannot be supported by evidence. In short, we want this thought-world of his to be an integral part of his whole life in which each addition that may come will be examined as it is acquired.

We have spoken many times of the different ways of knowing, and have insisted that the student must become acquainted with the most important of them. The students who come to us will possess the initial desire to know, for they would not otherwise have come. We must cultivate this desire, broaden it, deepen it, and give it the means of greatest possible realization.

At the beginning of his college course *we must lead each student to see the danger that will come to his full understanding and appreciation if he allows any way of inquiry to be blocked for him.* This is a very difficult part of education and, incidentally, one not recognized at all by many educators, who seem satisfied if their students show an interest in the one thing that they themselves are teaching. The task of keeping the ways of inquiry open becomes more difficult as enthusiasm for knowing becomes stronger, for enthusiasms usually have their accompanying blindnesses. A man becomes interested in one particular way of knowing, say the way of historical investigation. His interest becomes enthusiasm; enthusiasm leads to a commitment to that way of knowing as a life's vocation; commitment results in lack of interest in other ways of knowing, and leads finally to a contemptuous rejection of them as valueless. The enthusiasm for one way of coming to know things has for that person blocked all the other roads to knowledge. This is not merely an imagined danger. It happens. It is the occupational disease of scholars, a disease that prevents so many of them from ever becoming wise.

In order that the incoming student may see the wisdom of keeping all possible ways of inquiry open he must be shown very soon, and with all possible pedagogical effectiveness, certain basic psychological attitudes and preferences which lead men on to know and at the same time almost automatically limit the scope of their knowing. He must be led to understand that the fundamental assumptions based on these attitudes and preferences are effective for discovery but not effective in a use often made of them: the denial of what someone else claims to have discovered. To see this is of supreme importance for the young student.

There are two attitudes of mind in the search for truth, one or the other of which is almost inevitably present whenever someone tries seriously to investigate a given situation: the attitude of rigor and the attitude of receptiveness.

For the person holding the former attitude Ockham's razor shaves close, sometimes almost cutting the throat. The great aim is to exclude from what is accepted anything that has the least likelihood of being false, even anything that is superfluous. A test of what can be accepted as undeniably true is set up, and everything that fails to meet this test is rejected. The burden of proof is on the affirmative. A person who has this attitude would much rather miss something true than accept something false. "Better than ten innocent men are hanged than that one guilty man should go free." Rigorous thinking is characteristic of the organizational side of the sciences. It leads to the building of systems. The truth that it attains is accepted with great assurance. *But it has limitations. It can easily miss something true and valuable, and therefore it cannot claim to be the sole means of discovering what is true.* Moreover, it usually carries with it the logical error of assuming to be false that which cannot be proved true by its test. This means that the attitude of rigor, although it has been very fruitful in discovery, cannot escape being narrow in itself, and that the mind formed exclusively by it, regardless of its brilliance, is also narrow. We must try to prevent our student from committing himself solely to this attitude.

Rigorous thinking is more prevalent than we may suppose. We find it at the beginning of "modern" thinking in the method of Descartes, where the test of clarity and distinctness is demanded of everything that is to be accepted as true, and we find it also in the system of the logical positivists where empirical verifiability is demanded of everything that can be called meaningful. The historian is thinking rigorously when he rejects what is recorded only in doubtful sources. A rigorous thinker is logically justified in saying, "This I have found to be true by my method of investigation." He is not justified in saying, "What cannot be established as true by my method is false." And yet a famous biologist has recently said that theology is not knowledge because not one single principle of it can be established by the "scientific method."

If the attitude of rigor inclines a person to reject everything that can possibly be false, the attitude of receptiveness inclines another to accept everything that can possibly be true. He does not want to miss anything, and would rather allow some untruth to slip into his thought-world than to run the risk of excluding anything that happens to be true. "Better that ten guilty men go free than that one innocent man is hanged." The burden of proof is on the negative.

Knowledge acquired under the inspiration of this attitude will always be suspect but will quite possibly contain elements of valuable insight which the rigorist misses, insight which may lead to the understanding of things—even the things that the rigorist is dealing with—which the rigorist himself can never attain.

The attitude of receptiveness can operate in all the ways of knowing, at least in their advanced investigations and speculations. In the sciences, what is found by this receptivity is subject to rigorous systematic thinking where much is rejected and the rest ordered into a system. There remains then the possibility that what is rejected from the system may still be true. It can perhaps be ordered into another system, another science. But it can still be true even if every attempt to order it is unsuccessful, even if it cannot be included in any science.

Of the great realities to be known there is scientific knowledge, rigorously ordered and tested, and also a great mass of other knowledge—what the Greeks called opinion—which can be true but not so easily proved true. Yet this opinion is not accepted altogether without criticism or testing. It has been tested by such rather loose criteria as fittingness, beauty, usefulness, custom, common consent, and all the thousand and one subtle or unsubtle canons of acceptance that the *esprit de finesse* knows how to use, and use with great effectiveness, in successfully estimating and calculating in life's situations. This opinion is not science, but it can be, and everyone believes that at least some of it is, true.

One of the first things that our student must be led to realize, then, if the way of inquiry is not to be blocked for him, is that *scientific* and *true* are not synonymous terms. But he must also be led to realize that *scientific* and *worthy of interest* are not contrary terms. There is among our intellectuals, perhaps as a reaction from the popularity of science in the public imagination, a very articulate group who are professional despisers of the rigor and precision of science. Their sole-defenders-of-the-higher-values attitude is very attractive to some of the most intelligent students, who delight in stating that whether a certain event actually took place or not is of no importance, that "sitting down before a fact and observing it" is stultifying to the intellect, and that the creative mind can allow no distinction between fact and fancy. The lively intelligence, the urbanity, and above all the beautiful rhetoric of some of these people hide from many men an appalling narrowness which would reject with contempt much of the intellectual accomplishment of the human race.

The doctor of philosophy who would steer his students past this danger will in some way have to lead them to see that there is a valuable activity of the intellect in which fancy and imagination lead to insights and beauties which could not be discovered without them, and that there is an equally valuable activity of the intellect in which the play of fancy and imagination must be reduced to as near nothing as possible. The student may prefer one of these ways to the other, but he must respect them both if he is ever to attain wisdom.

If the student is to be freed from bondage to a particular attitude of mind, he is also to be freed from bondage to time—either to the present or the past—and must neither worship the term *modern* nor hold it in contempt. The sociologist Sorokin has poured scorn on the "New Columbuses" who triumphantly announce their discovery of what has been known for a couple of milleniums. But there are also men who apparently believe that discoveries stopped some time before Columbus, that everything worth while that we know can be traced back to the Greeks (if they are of one persuasion) or to St. Thomas Aquinas (if they are of another). But to commit one's thinking to the ways of one particular historical age is narrowness.

It might seem that the hardest task of the doctor of philosophy in this situation is to break the shell of modernity from around the student so that he can respect the genuine accomplishments of ancient and medieval thinking. This would probably be the best procedure with the greater number of young people, but there are always some, and these not the least intelligent of the group, who very quickly surround themselves with the shell of antiquity. Once the glory of Plato flashes on a person's mind the dazzle often prevents his ever seeing any other glory. Emerson has said, "Plato is philosophy and philosophy Plato." This is narrowness no matter how succinct the aphorism.

We have mentioned the attitudes of rigor and receptiveness as attitudes influencing the thinking of almost all of us. But there are certain other attitudes or preferences that influence our thinking and make that thinking different from the thought of other times. If the student can understand these he can perhaps be saved from bondage to any age, because he can then see that the characteristic thinking of each age has certain blind sides which block the way of inquiry in some directions.

In every period there are certain questions that interest people and certain others that they do not ask. There are some kinds of proof that are accepted and other kinds that leave them unconvinced. Each age has its own idea of what a *satisfactory* explanation is. Someone has said that the change from Aristotelian to modern physics came when people stopped asking "Why is this thing moving?" and began to ask "Why has this thing stopped moving?" Both of these questions are legitimate, but one age prefers one question, another age the other. The Platonists demanded that what they would include in knowledge, as distinct

85

from opinion, must be proved by a quasi-mathematical demonstration. They were quite unimpressed by the inductive reasoning that Francis Bacon later hailed as the basic thinking of natural science. In Aristotelian science no explanation was complete without the final cause—the answer to the question, "Where is it tending?" or "What is it for?" In modern science (except biology) no one thinks of asking that question. In medieval thinking, a complete explanation always led back to the first cause. Much modern knowledge has been organized with a view to dispensing with divine causation.

Modern thinking, born as it was out of a reaction against traditional western thought, has always had "debunking" as one of its main tendencies. It has all too easily refused to follow many ways of inquiry. If a man would be wise, this bias toward the negative must be taken into account when dealing with modern thinkers, and recognized for what it is. A habit of thought has no claim to be permanently valuable beyond others.

When the student once realizes that most thinking is ruled by what might be called contemporary (and temporary) fashion, and that the fashion changes from age to age, he can perhaps manage to accept what he finds valuable in the thinking of every age without committing himself so completely to the way of thinking of any of them that he sees no value in thinking in another way. He may become able to examine every age, including his own, with both positive and negative criticism.

This investigation of the subjective situation underlying human thinking is absolutely necessary for a young person who is starting out in the intellectual life, if he is to have a chance of becoming a wise and understanding man. He must see that every age, and every system of thought, has built into its intellectual structure various blockades preventing inquiry in some directions. If he is to become wise, and develop his capacities to the full, he must learn not to accept these blockades but to look beyond them. If he does not understand this he will, as he advances, inevitably fall into the besetting affliction of intellectuals.

* * *

9

When the student has gained the preliminary recognitions mentioned in the last chapter, he will be able to study the different ways in which people come to know some things without being so intrigued by one that he has no respect for or understanding of others. He can regard each way of knowing as *a* way, not *the* way, and therefore he can investigate all the ways that he can discover, with the confidence that in each he will find something that increases his knowledge, and perhaps also his understanding and wisdom.

In beginning the investigation of the ways of knowing one is immediately met with the fact that much of what we know is accepted on some kind of authority. It is by the acceptance of someone else's word that most of our knowledge begins, and this is more true of the educated than of the uneducated person; for the initial intellectual expansion through education consists in substituting for one's limited experience the authority of teachers and books. Even in college most of what students come to accept is text-book knowledge, and the majority of "good students" are simply well-informed men. Most of the history, the economics, the natural science and the theology that they know is on the informational level, with sometimes a standard "reason why," also authoritative, added in explanation. It is learned by being committed to memory (witness the cramming before examinations). The student does not discover these truths, and he does not get to know them with the kind of knowing that was used in their discovery and in their initial acceptance as true. They are still in the realm of opinion for him. It is only in mathematics that the text-books, in their very presentation of problems, abdicate their authority and lead the student to arrive at his conclusions by his own thinking and in a certain sense to become a discoverer.

Reliance on the authority of the expert is a way of knowing that the student will never altogether transcend. He can never make a thorough investigation of everything that he accepts. But he can learn to adopt a critical attitude toward the statements of experts, realizing that, as the medieval philosophers insisted, a position based upon authority is scientifically very weak. He should know, for instance, that the expert often makes statements outside the field in which he is an authority, and that these statements do not bear a trace of whatever authority he may have. And it is most necessary, and a key to much understanding, for the student to realize that when the expert leaves the details of his special knowledge and deals with the fundamental propositions and psychological preferences upon which his knowledge has been built, he has then come out from behind the shield of his expertness, and the ordinary man can meet him on common ground. The ordinary man or the student can examine these propositions and preferences with his own logic and can give a respectable opinion as to their validity. Thus the student will develop a certain confidence in the presence of "authority." Above all he will come to see the unreliability of such general pronouncements as "Science teaches . . ." or "Educators tell us . . ."

The student will have an additional means of defense against the tyranny of experts outside their fields, for he will see the limitations of the methods that they use. He will be aware of what can be known by these methods and what cannot. He will thus be able to approach authoritative statements critically.

It is essential that the wise and understanding man will never be satisfied with remaining simply well-informed. He will want to get behind the authoritative statement to find the reason why, to share in some measure the discovery that gave rise to the statement. If he cannot get behind it, at least he wants to "see" with the authority as much as possible, to enter with him into his way of thinking so as to understand that what he says is to be trusted. It is to this getting behind the authorities or seeing with them that we wish to lead our students. It is an essential task for the teacher. We will take the authorities as our partners in this enterprise. They will become teachers with us—not masters but teachers—by means of what they have written or what has been written of them. One of the best ways to gain an understanding of a way of knowing is to study the work of a man who has pioneered or gone far in that way.

In our western tradition the first realized way of coming to know, the way used by those who first developed an interest in knowing for knowing's sake, came to be called *dialectic*. It has been greatly esteemed in our past but has in more recent times fallen into disrepute, although those who argue against its value often make use of it in their argument.

In dialectic you come to know by "thinking things out," usually in discussion with others, relying on the power of thought without recourse to continued observation or experiment or any other single method of operation. In dialectic as in mathematics you start with something which all agree to accept, define the concepts you are going to use, and go on from there; but in dialectic you not only agree to *assume* that certain fundamental propositions are true; you have a firm conviction that they *are* true. And certain of these truths with which you start are value judgments that seem to be deeply ingrained in the human being; that unity is better than disunity, that harmony is better than discord, order better than disorder, the permanent better than the transient, success better than failure, meaningfulness better than meaninglessness. Most of the ethical, social and political theory upon which our modern society is based has been erected by dialectical thinking. Read the Federalist Papers as an example.

If the student is to break his hard shell of modernity and appreciate the thinking of the past, he must become familiar with the dialectic, at least so far as to follow its reasoning without pulling back at every step because the thinking is not empirical. He must look at the structure without prejudice, and only when he has understood it should he pass judgment on it. To be unable to follow the reasoning of Socrates or Aristotle is to be ignorant. To be unwilling to do so is to be narrow. To be either is to impoverish one's intellectual life.

Dialectical thinking comes easily to the person who has not been inoculated against it, and the student should be introduced to it and spend time in it before being introduced to its modern critics. And he should also be shown that the critics are using it in their arguments against it, for every person who tries to show that one method of attaining truth is better than another uses dialectic to prove his point. The man who holds that the empirical test for truth is the only valid test has to show *why* the empirical test is so valuable. When he is showing this he is not thinking empirically; he is thinking dialectically. He is using value judgments. He is going from the *is* to the *ought*.

The ancient dialectician knew he was thinking dialectically. He knew the difference between dialectic and demonstration. The modern critic of dialectic does not know that in formulating and justifying his methodological starting point (which unconsciously becomes for him an ontological starting point) he is using dialectic, and usually metaphysics too. If our student is to become a wise man, dialectical thinking must not be neglected in his education.

When we have shown the general conditions and limitations of all ways of thinking, and have called the student's attention to the place and the limitations of authority in knowing, we will assign reading and involve him in discussion of the Greek and Latin philosophical and moral classics, so that he will become familiar with this way of thinking and will gain from it some fundamental knowledge of man, society, and the world. He will also learn a way of approaching problems and will not suffer from an *a priori* unwillingness to make moral judgments in existential situations.

The two systems of knowledge which developed dialectically quite early in our tradition are metaphysics and ethics. Metaphysical thinking is a way of coming to understanding which is even more out of fashion than is the parent dialectic itself. The word *metaphysics* has been so long out of scientific repute that it has been appropriated by an assortment of propagandists, its disrepute has grown, and the ridicule has kept pace with the disrepute. "Metaphysics is searching in an absolutely dark room for a black cat that isn't there." "Metaphysics is a constant misuse of a terminology expressly created for that purpose." Or, less ridiculing but more serious, "Metaphysics is completely meaningless."

But since we are trying to educate men and not striving to keep pace with fashion, we will not be too much concerned with the current opinion of this field of knowledge. If academic fashion and the opinion of leading scholars ignores a kind of knowledge and a way of thinking that we believe to be necessary for a more complete understanding of things, we will teach that knowledge and that way of thinking, realizing that academic fashion is fleeting and that great contemporary scholars are to be respected for what they have discovered and are to be listened to when they speak about it. They are not to be respected for their ignorance or listened to in their denials.

We will therefore introduce the student to the distinction between what exists and our knowledge of it, between *being* and *being perceived*. We will lead him to sort out the different meanings that he has in his mind when he uses the word *is*, and to come to some conclusion about what the ultimate state of things must be if we discover new facts about "something," or correct one another's ideas about "something." We will examine the most basic distinctions between things that are, and consider how they are like each other and how unlike. We will discuss the possibility of there being something that we cannot perceive with any of our senses, and whether this something is to be inferred from what we do perceive.

When the student has come to some of these fundamental metaphysical conclusions he will be able as he advances in knowledge to integrate that knowledge into one thought-world because he has already seen that the things of which he has the knowledge are integrated into one universe of being. And he will have the further advantage of being able to integrate his new knowledge with the experience of his daily life, so that he is not pulled apart by the opposition of his theoretical learning to the assumptions that he must make if he is to act.

Closely allied with metaphysics in its rising out of the ancient dialectic is the science of ethics. This is a sustained and serious effort to derive an *ought* from an *is*, to show how by thinking alone, unsupported by divine revelation or the testimony of custom, one can determine from the very nature of a given existential situation what one's duty is in that situation, and how principles of conduct can be determined which are valid even though not universally acknowledged.

Nothing could be farther from the prevailing relativism than this kind of thinking, yet the world has not been entirely at ease

91

in its relativism. It looks longingly for something to replace the traditional values that it has lost. For the purpose of statesmanship as well as for the ordering of one's own life there is need of renewed thinking along the lines of the old science of ethics. Such thinking has not been proved invalid; it has simply gone out of fashion, and with it has gone the possibility of the intellectual establishment of the principles upon which our society is based.

The college must not let the case for ethical thinking go by default. The student must become familiar with, for instance, Plato's argument which attempts to show that it is better to be just than unjust even when no advantage other than being just is gained thereby. It is only when he knows the argument that he can be reasonable in his rejection of it if he should decide to reject it.

There is no place where theory impinges more directly upon living than right here. If the men who have received the higher education have never arrived at the reasoned conviction that one has the obligation to act justly even when no policeman is in sight, then we are not a political society but a rabble, uncontrollable except by coercion. It would seem that our very existence as a society depends on the revitalizing of ethical thinking in such a way as to bring it into fashion. Where can this be done better than in the dialogue of a college?

The ancient sciences constructed by dialectic are so long out of fashion that we have had to make a point of explaining why we insist in including them in higher education. In the fields of knowledge that we are now going to discuss there will be (until we get to the last one) no need of explaining why we include them, but some need of explaining the way in which we will deal with them.

Thomas Aquinas has said that mathematical knowing is the kind of knowing most suited to the human mind, and this assertion seems to be borne out by the thinkers who find a great satisfaction when they have succeeded in bringing their field of knowledge under some mathematical system. There is a satisfying clarity about, say, a demonstration in geometry. When you have followed the reasoning of this demonstration to its conclusion, you really know that conclusion. It is not just opinion; it is *knowledge.* You really understand why the conclusion is true; you see that it could not be otherwise. There are no shadows. You think that if our knowledge of everything could be like this, how heavenly it would be.

Besides the clarity of mathematics there is its precision. Each term that is used is strictly defined. Each symbol has one meaning and one alone. You know exactly what you mean in every step of the thinking, and you can show another person exactly what you mean. There are no equivocations, not even any connotations beyond what is clearly stated in the definitions. There are no hidden assumptions. The whole rational process is out in plain sight. And by this clear and precise thinking you get somewhere. You can come to know what you did not know before. It will be a great disaster to the student's intellectual integrity if he does not become familiar with these sciences.

But in spite of mathematics being suited to the human mind in the abstract, we do not need Pascal's testimony that the *esprit de geometrie* is not possessed by everybody to convince us that there are some intelligent people whose minds simply do not handle mathematical thinking well. Students of this sort should not be compelled to go far in it, or be judged by their progress in it; but they must not be allowed to ignore it. Every effort must be made to lead them to see and understand the kind of thinking that goes on in the mathematical field, and to respect it even if they do not like it.

To those who do well in mathematics our college must provide opportunity to go far. But if there is to be full development of their mental power they must not be allowed to be so preoccupied by this fascinating subject that they fail to appreciate other ways in which the mind can come to know. The very precision and clarity of mathematical thinking make it easy for those who love it to ignore other ways of arriving at the truth.

It is hardly possible for one to be merely a well-informed man in mathematics. The why's and wherefore's are a part of the subject. But there is nothing easier than to be merely well informed in the natural sciences. There is of course a basic fund of scientific information which every man must possess if he is to fit into the modern world. He should know, for instance, what the second law of thermodynamics is. But he can have this information on authority without ever entering into the realm of science as a way of knowing, without ever understanding the spirit that inspires scientific investigation or the methods by which it is carried on, and without ever appreciating the greatness of the human accomplishment in building a science. If the student is to understand the world of thought at all, however, he must go beyond the informational level and come to appreciate what natural science is. The ordinary way of teaching science to a non-specialist frequently fails altogether in leading beyond information.

A student in a laboratory has a microscope and a text-book. The microscope is focused on a slide upon which paramecia are coursing around in a drop of water. There is a drawing of a paramecium in the book. The student is to draw what he sees, but what he sees is somewhat confused because the animals will not stand still. So, having confidence that the author of the text-book knows what a paramecium looks like, the student copies the drawing in the book, even though, as far as he can see, it resembles the real paramecium very little. His drawing is accepted by the instructor and everyone is happy. But the student has learned nothing of scientific investigation. He has done no scientific thinking, and made no discovery. The observation-corrected-by-text-book method is clearly not the one to use if we are serious about science.

In the time at the student's disposal for the study of natural science he must be led as far as possible into the heart of it. He must do what scientists do. Thus he must have experience in observing carefully and checking his observations, describing accurately what he has observed, seeking similarities, relationships and regularities and "putting nature to the question" by experiment. This activity and the thinking that arises from it need not be the same for all students. If a student shows an interest in one line of scientific inquiry he will learn more by following that interest through observation, description, inference and experiment that by going through a course of study prescribed for everyone.

In the community of learning those teachers especially interested in natural science will be conducting experiments to add to their own knowledge, and part of the exciting life of the community will be found in the interest of the students in these experiments—in watching what the teacher is doing, in questioning him, arguing and making suggestions. There could well be some scientists in residence in the community whose sole teaching function would consist in doing their scientific investigating in public.

The student must be kept constantly aware that natural science is knowledge *about something,* and that something is the things that make up the physical universe. Therefore, as we have said before, there must be constant referring of science to things, so that the connection will never be forgotten. Since in our modern world of concrete, steel and glass it is with inanimate things that people have most contact, the school will have to make a special effort to bring the student into relation with living things. Field work in the biological sciences must have an important place among the activities of the community.

In addition to getting into the realm of science by doing what scientists do and thinking the way they think and reading about them and their work, some time must be spent on the philosophical side of science. What, for instance, is a scientific theory, a law, a species? What is the realm of applicability of scientific thinking? How is mathematics related to natural science? Are there other ways of knowing the same things that natural science deals with? If the student is to be wise he must have done some thinking along these lines, at least so far as to realize that there are problems here. We must not let him become so entranced with the thought and the practice *within* science that he becomes unable to think of it as only a part of the whole of knowing.

A knowledge of history gives another dimension to our understanding of things, especially human things. It shows us how they came to be what they are, and therefore puts them in perspective. Political institutions, for instance, could scarcely be understood at all if only their existing structure were examined and not the historical process that gave rise to them.

Historical knowledge is a knowledge of what happened in the human affairs of the past, and a great part of what happened is what the people of the past thought and felt, and why they did what they did. It is much more than a bare chronological sketch of past events. In order to possess it a person must be able to "live into" past situations. The good historian persuades his readers to enter into the life and thought of the past and gives them an understanding not only of those times but, indirectly, of their own time.

A student does not get this historical insight by reading brief surveys of long periods of the past. He gets it by accompanying a good teacher or author in a detailed study of periods or situations which the teacher or author has himself "lived into." The periods to be investigated by the student in our community, therefore, will depend on the particular interests of the teachers who are at any given time desirous of teaching history. Once the student has learned with the help of the teacher how to proceed, he can study other periods on his own. The kind of historical knowledge that one gains from a brief survey of a long period is valuable as information, but such knowledge can easily be got from reading at any time of life. There is no need to take up the school's time with it. A survey of history supplies a valuable frame-work for relating and integrating chronologically all the knowledge that the student possesses and will possess. It is important to know what comes before what. As a way of ordering knowledge it is effective only after there is considerable knowledge to order; and only when there is considerable knowledge to hang on this historical frame-work will the frame-work itself be easily remembered. This is a good reason for postponing the historical survey until later, and making it an important part of one's reading program after leaving college.

Historical knowledge can give a valuable insight into human affairs only if it is an accurate representation of the past, both in recording the events and in its account of the thought and intention that accompanied the events. Consequently the student must be given an understanding of the historical method. He must know how the historical investigator seeks evidence, how he uses it, what his criteria for accepting evidence are, and what kind of certainty can be expected for his finished work. It is only by such understanding that a person who reads history can be freed from dependence on the authority of some historian who happens to appeal to him. Historical writing is so fascinating to some people (and I include myself among them) and the conclusions of different historians about the same situation in the past are so different, that if a person is to maintain his autonomy he must be prepared to read history with at least a minimum of critical ability.

Following our usual practice of not letting enthusiasm run away with our people, we must be careful to let them see that the historical development of an institution, a society or a custom is not all that can be known about it, that it can also be approached by way of description or evaluation, and that therefore historicism offers an inadequate view of things.

A competent historian once told me about a lecture he had attended which was given by a literary critic. He was disturbed by what seemed to him an irresponsible use of words in the address. The speaker employed words in such a way that if one gave each word its conventional dictionary meaning the message did not make sense. The historian concluded that the lecture was without value. The incident exemplifies, of course, the narrowness of some competent scholars. But it also shows the essential difference between the scientific use of words and poetic use, and one of the differences between science in general and imaginative literature.

People primarily interested in science will frequently explain poetry as an appeal to the emotions. It stirs you up, makes you happy, makes you tingle with love for your country, sends you out to shoot somebody, or puts you in a mood to shoot yourself. Poetry may also be regarded, condescendingly, as a pretty accomplishments, to be applauded in the *salons*. This is Descartes' view of it, and apparently also Pascal's. The vulgar view of poetry as something not very important is expressed in the popular saying: "There's more truth than poetry in that."

But poetry, together with the rest of imaginative literature, is an enrichment of knowledge, every bit as enriching as science. It affects the emotions, of course, but its communication is also, and more importantly, intellectual. It gives insights, appreciations, and nuances of seeing that one would not get otherwise, and it enables one to understand things not understood before. Some of

97

the wisdom gained in poetry can be described in words; but some of it can be explained only by acknowledging that as a result of poetry something has happened to you that has made you a better and more understanding man. This can also happen as a result of experience with the other fine arts.

Imaginative literature and the arts must have an important role in the life of our community of learning. Our traditional American culture has been quite unreceptive to the message of art, and we will have to make a special effort to lead our students to discover it. The students will do much reading of great literature and there will be if possible an artist in residence whose teaching will consist in doing his work with students watching and asking questions.

Discussion of works of art and the problems of artistic creation will be prominent in the formal dialogue, and it will be carried on, of course, in the informal dialogue that follows. Students will be encouraged to try their own hand at creating something. It is easier to appreciate the master's skill when you yourself have tried your hand at a craft.

Some years ago I visited a small college in Kentucky. There was an elderly man there, an Austrian, who as resident artist was a kind of Leonardo da Vinci in his versatility. His specialty was calligraphy, but he was also a painter, a sculptor and an architect, and to round off his accomplishments he had just made himself a spinet and played it with enthusiasm. This man had enchanted the whole college and everyone from the president to the lowliest freshman was working at painting. I never saw in a student body such a high level of appreciation of the task of the artist. The informal work of this man accomplished more than any amount of class work could possibly have done.

There is no kind of knowing against which the what-I-don't-know-is-not-knowledge mentality stands so firmly opposed as it stands against knowing by faith. Modern thinking originated in a rebellion against late medieval theology and philosophy, and rebellion, even though it has its justifications, often narrows the mind of the rebels, making it difficult for them to see any value in the system against which they are rebelling. One born and brought up in this anti-theological tradition rarely gives to theology that fair hearing which was asked of, but not granted by, the

98

theologians in an earlier day. It is time now that young people should again be given access to a way along which many men of no small intellectual capacity have travelled. Here again, as in the case of metaphysics, our college must break with contemporary academic tradition in order to give people a higher education.

The distinctive way of knowing theological truth, although other ways are of course employed in a subsidiary fashion, is the way of revelation: revealed truth appropriated to the individual person by faith. Therefore the fundamental subject of study will be the nature of faith and the content of revelation. But the acceptance of revealed truth about God and man has repercussions everywhere. The person who has thus believed will never look at anything in quite the same way as an unbeliever looks at it. That is why theology is so important. It brings with it a world view and an enlightenment.

If this is true, and millions believe that it is, then the teacher who has received this enlightenment can no more refuse to try to lead his students to it than a man who has seen the glory of science can be restrained from sharing it.

And here is the anomoly of the contemporary situation. We regard a certain body of truth as public—mathematics, natural science, social science, literature, etc. And then there is religious truth, if it be truth, which is a purely private concern. But every truth is private in the sense that it is assented to by each individual separately and privately, if it is assented to at all; and there is no truth which does not have its dissenters. In many fields of knowledge there are widely opposed schools of thought, and much is taught by some which is believed false by others. There is not much in common, for instance, between the views of history held by Karl Marx and by Thomas Carlyle. It is true that theology is unique in the way in which it is known, but so are mathematics and history. Theology gives a *Weltanschauung,* but so do history and physics if they are taken as the ultimate view of things, and so does scepticism. Theology is communicable and therefore public. Its propositions can be discussed and accepted or rejected by its criteria of truth.

As Newman said a century ago, when theology is not officially recognized as a legitimate body of knowledge, that does not mean that theological statements are not made. It means that they are made irresponsibly by people who have not had sufficient experience in the subject to be able to distinguish profundity from absurdity. We mentioned before that a distinguished biologist has said that theology cannot be valid knowledge because not one of its propositions is established by the scientific method. And another scientist a few years ago assured his students that there could not be such a thing as a soul because the human body weighed just the same after death as before.

We have now discussed the principal ways of knowing, not to explain them as much as to show how we will introduce our students to them. The ways of knowing are not synonymous with the fields of knowledge. In every field of knowledge several ways of knowing are employed. The social sciences, for instance, use the way of natural science, the way of history, the way of mathematics, etc. All fields of knowledge use the way of dialectic not only in establishing the validity of their methods and first principles but very often in the internal procedure of developing the field. Most of the thinkers in every field assume some kind of metaphysics, though some of them are not aware of it. When the student understands the ways in which men come to know things he has a good instrument for learning to feel at home in the fields of knowledge that he may care to enter.

As we said in an earlier chapter, knowledge is knowledge *about* something; it is our means of coming into intellectual contact with what is. By the mere study and practice of the ways of knowing the student comes to know quite a lot about things. It is very necessary, because of the short time spent in college, that what he comes to know are the important things rather than the irrelevant or the superficial things. In the four great realities to be known—man, society, the universe and God—some things are central and illuminating, some things are relatively unimportant. Care will be taken that the reading, discussion, lectures, and all the pedagogical methods and practices of the community will direct the student to the central things. At the end of his time there he will not only know, and know how he knows, but he will have a firm intellectual foundation for the knowledge he will acquire in later life. His college course will thus be the beginning of his education rather than the completion of it.

* * *

10

In this country we have an established pattern of higher education, a pattern which has so soaked into our national thinking that it seems to us to be a part of the nature of things. If we want to be educated we work for a degree. We get this degree by assembling the right number and the right kind of credits. Credits are given for courses that are passed, and are simply a convenient means of keeping track of the courses and their relative quantitative value. Each course deals with a particular aspect of the knowledge we are seeking (or the knowledge our institution prescribes for us even though we are not seeking it.) Most of the schemes for improving higher education take this pattern for granted, and concern themselves with trying to make it work better.

But it is our contention that the pattern itself is one of the principal things wrong with higher education, and every scheme of reform which keeps the pattern guarantees its own failure. It is for this reason that we have devise an altogether different pattern for our community of learning.

Walter Bagehot has said that one of the reasons for the decline of states is that there has been, imbedded in their constitutions, some way of doing things, some cherished value, some institution, which strangles them. The people may love this thing, whatever it is. Theorists may demand it. But it is fatal.

One example of this kind of self-destruction would be, I suggest, the established ideal of the classical world that a free man should do no menial work. Another would be the medieval custom of giving land to support the officials appointed by the king to enforce civic order. The ownership of the land made the official independent of the authority of the king who gave the land, and thus encouraged him to become a part of the very anarchy that he was appointed to suppress. It has also been said that the institution of proportional representation, so attractive theoretically, has been the ruin of the twentieth century democracies that have adopted it.

In the American system of higher education the course-and-credit system has that drive to extinction. As the pattern or form in which higher education is given it frustrates the essential aims of such education. It stands as an effectual barrier against the integration of knowledge, against the seeing of relations, against independent thinking, and against the uniquely personal relations which must subsist between each teacher and each student if the teaching-learning process is to go on successfully.

This pattern can be accounted for historically. In every society there are certain prevailing forms under which human enterprise is organized. Their effectiveness in one kind of enterprise commends them for universal use, so that they are extended far beyond the range where they have much relevance to the work that is to be done. For instance, in the towns of medieval Europe the craft guild supplied the form under which men got together to do things. This pattern gave them their organization for making and selling shoes—and it went on to give them their organization for teaching the liberal arts in the universities. In our day two such forms are very popular, and supply ways of organizing innumerable activities. One of these forms is the parliamentary meeting. We get things done by appointing a chairman and a secretary, and then by proposing, discussing and passing motions. If an action results from this pattern it seems to us much more valid than if it is carried out informally with an "All right, let's get going" attitude.

Another popular form of organization is the factory. Extremely successful for the making of things, it has usually been rather unfortunate in its effect on the human beings working there. Two key ideas stand out in this way of organizing human activity. The first is the idea of the division of labor. The whole process of making something is divided into the different kinds of action involved, and each of these kinds of action is assigned to persons particularly trained in it. If one expert leaves, another, similarly trained, takes his place, and the process is not interrupted. The thing as it is being made passes from one of these experts to another until all that needs to be done to it is done, and it emerges a finished product.

The second idea is that of standard interchangeable parts for standard uniform products. Discovered perhaps by Eli Whitney and brought to perfection by Henry Ford, this idea makes possible the manufacture of parts for a product in widely separated places, the assembly of them anywhere according to standard blueprints, and the repair of the product everywhere. There is no question but that things can be made more quickly and more cheaply and more abundantly when these two ideas dominate the manufacturing process.

There are certain underlying assumptions and practices in the employment of these ideas which appear to hold good whether we speak of cars, guns or radios. They may be stated thus:

1. Parts built to the same specifications will be the same, whether made in New York or San Francisco, whether made by Joe Smith or Juan Mendoza.

2. The whole is equal to the sum of all its parts. If, for example, all the necessary parts of a car are put together correctly, you have a car.

3. If a part is missing or defective, install the missing part or replace the defective part and you have a satisfactory car again.

4. You ascertain that a car is satisfactory by an inspection to see if all the parts are there and operating as they should.

5. If you wish, you can make several standard models of your car. You simply have to draw up several plans, varying the parts (all of them standard in their type) so that the assembled totals will be different, but each one standard according to its specifications.

All these assumptions are quantitative. The problems in which they are relevant are problems of addition, subtraction, combination and re-combination. They are the kind of problems easily handled by a computer, and whose results can be dealt with by a filing clerk.

But these assumptions do not hold with human beings, whose problems are not of this kind; and when they are applied to a human situation such as education, they frustrate every intelligent human purpose.

Let us see how closely our course-and-credit system of education follows the form of the factory. The student, when he has registered in a college, is put on the assembly line, which conveys him past a number of expert teachers, each one of whom supplies him with a course. The passed course, with its accompanying credits, is the part attached to him, and like the part, if it is attached correctly (this the teacher ascertains by examination), it remains firmly fixed no matter what happens. Each course is standard of its kind. Any teacher who is qualified as an expert can give the course, can attach the part. The student need not even know the teacher's name, for it makes no difference who he is. If necessary the student can be taken off the assembly line in Maine and shipped, along with his records in terms of credits, to California and put on an assembly line there, where the courses not already attached can be put on. Everything is standard. He can be assembled anywhere. When an inspection of records shows that all the necessary courses have been attached, the degree is stamped on him and he is educated. Our whole society accepts him as such and everyone is happy.

No one asks, "What does this man know of history?" They ask, "What courses in history has he taken?" Prospective employers and graduate schools want to see a transcript of his courses and grades. They don't try to find out what has happened to the student's mind during his years in college. They don't ask if he can think, or if he is wise and understanding. They want something they can measure, and the condition of the mind is not subject to quantitative evaluation. So they measure something else and think they are measuring a mind. Because of the quantitative standard involved in the course-and-credit system the whole academic world has moved into an illusion, measuring what cannot be measured, striving for and applauding values which have little to do with education, and raising requirements which become simply hindrances to a person's real educational development.

The assumptions of the system are inhuman. Knowledge is a continuum. If it is divided into parts and parcels it dies. There is no such thing as a "field" of knowledge delimited in such a way that a student can think right up to the edge of it and then stop thinking, or in such a way that an expert can teach right up to the edge with full authority, and then lose all authority if he steps over the edge, or in such a way that a person who is not a certified expert cannot enter it with any authority at all. The concept of both knowledge and thinking is falsely represented to the student by the system.

When a teacher and a group of students study together regularly over a period of time, all of them undergo an educational experience that is unique. It may be more or less valuable, but it is not a thing that can be standardized. When another teacher meets with other students quite a different experience takes place, even though the course is the same according to the catalog. Therefore it is a misrepresentation to the student and to the world to pretend that having taken a course is equivalent to knowing something or being able to think profitably in a certain area. It is a mistake to assume that when two students have taken the same course they have equivalent knowledge, or that when two teachers teach the same course the same thing happens to both groups of students.

These are only some of the theoretical objections to the course-and-credit system in higher education (or any education). There are also great practical objections.

There is a kind of Gresham's Law of Education to the effect that bad academic practices tend to drive out good ones. The course-and-credit system is bad academic practice, and it is very effective in driving out good practices that may spring up from time to time in institutions where it holds sway.

I suppose that every teacher who has taught for any length of time has had the experience of working with a few students in some private investigation or study. Sometimes such activity provides a wonderful educational experience for the students. Some of them may be coming intellectually alive for the first time. Everyone concerned is interested and learning something. And the result? Pressure of course-work catches up with these students. They must pass their courses in order to graduate. They must get good grades in order to get into law school. This will take all their time, and they sadly give up the private study which they know to be the most profitable they have ever done, in order to meet the demands of the system.

This happens quite frequently. Because of the system we have two kinds of knowledge: that which "counts" and that which doesn't. The knowledge that counts is that which is relevant to a course that one is taking or will take—anything that can be relevantly introduced into the discussion or the examination. All other knowledge, however valuable it may be, and even though it is relevant to a course already taken, has no way of presenting itself for evaluation. There are students who do gain this extra-curricular knowledge and understanding. Some of them, be it said to their glory, even neglect their unprofitable courses in order to spend their time well. And their grades suffer.

The student who has an intense desire to know, and who follows this desire where he finds that he is best coming to know, regardless of his courses, will always suffer in his grades and thus in his standing in the school and before the world. More power to him! But there ought to be a system for him in which following the way of learning that is best for him will not be penalized.

We teachers often find exceptionally good students whose excellence is not at all reflected in the official records of the school. This leads us to wonder if true intellectual excellence is ever reflected in these records. Do the records reflect excellence or do they reflect merely a prudent conformity to a system?

And the teacher? If he is to be a true doctor of philosophy, is he also bound to neglect his courses if he finds that the students are learning more in some private educational activity which he is conducting than they are in his courses?

The course-and-credit system is sometimes defended because it makes certain duties of administration easier—that is, it makes things easier for the computer and the filing clerk. It makes possible a general uniformity which is sometimes even hailed as "justice to the student." The essence of justice, the argument runs, is uniformity of treatment. If you try to deal with each student in the way most suited to him, you do not treat all the students uniformly. Therefore you act unjustly. But this is ridiculous. Justice in education surely occurs when every teacher

106

does the very best he can for every student, and the best is never the same for any two students.

We factory-minded Americans are the only people in the world who have thought of using such a system in educating human beings. It is now time to devise a completely new way of doing things. The system cannot simply be modified, for if it is present at all it will destroy all other academic practice. It must be abolished root and branch if we are to have a true educational system.

* * *

11

It will be realized from our description of the community of learning that the community is presumed to be small. Smallness is essential to its being a genuine face-to-face community, and therefore it will be kept small as a matter of principle, with a maximum of perhaps two hundred students. This will allow all its members to come together in a meeting of not unmanageable size for the formal dialogue and for public exercises and celebrations. The small number of people concerned will also make it possible to change the whole program readily if it is desired to drop everything in order to hear and talk to a distinguished visitor, or to meet an emergency. The plan of education involves an elasticity of action that becomes almost impossible when large numbers are involved.

But, some will object, would not such a small institution be a most inefficient institution?

This leads us to a discussion of the costs of higher education. We have been informed by some highly respected educators that the price of excellence is high; and the Amerian public, perhaps reading the meaning of these educators correctly, has assumed that a high price means a lot of dollars, and that excellence can be bought with dollars. Thus education is entangled in the great Amerian heresy which teaches that problems can be solved by appropriating money.

We must make a distinction within the field that present-day higher education encompasses. Professional education is expensive, and society, if it wants professional experts—in medicine, in electronics, in computers, in nuclear science, in space mechanics, in economics, in historical investigation—must in some way meet the great expense of producing and sustaining them. In so far as these experts are needed, the expense is justified.

But the fundamental higher education that we have been describing is a different thing altogether. Here we are educating men, not training experts. We are educating them by drawing them into a community of learning and understanding, where human relationships are all-important. In such an institution the conditions differ from the conditions in a school for training professional experts, and consequently the economic principles involved are different. This has a great effect on the price of excellence in dollars.

There is an educational rule of inverse proportion: *The excellence of teaching and learning in an institution of higher liberal learning varies inversely with the elaborateness of the material equipment*. Men, both teachers and learners, may be overwhelmed by wonderful buildings and "the best" facilities. For one thing, the maintenance of all these things becomes a psychological burden which quenches the informality and spontaneity that is so valuable in education. It is like having a house so perfect that you are afraid to do anything in it.

There is a valid psychological reason for the bad effect of good equipment. When teachers and learners work together to contrive means of meeting materially adverse circumstances a comradeship develops and a real sense of community arises. This is the best possible learning environment, whereas when there is no necessity of contriving it often happens that no comradeship develops, and learning is handicapped.

That austerity is the proper climate for the human spirit seems to be a rather consistent teaching of our tradition. An abundance of material things lulls the mind if it does not corrupt it. Therefore anything resembling luxury is to be avoided in the educational environment not only because it is expensive but, more than this, because it is harmful. Our colleges, following instead of leading, have conformed to the prevalent American conception that the "good things of life" are comfort and a plentiful supply of gadgets. They honor the old-time ascetic heroes of education, but their practice is quite otherwise, and they submit to the demands of the students and their parents. They rejoice in their impressive buildings and carefully landscaped grounds tended by a staff of maintenance men. They insist upon facilities for all kinds of sport, with professional coaches. They encourage elaborate social events. Is it any wonder that even non-professional education is expensive?

But what is really needed for an institution of higher liberal learning? Students and teachers in community, and a place where they can meet. Nothing more.

The place can and should be simple—four walls and a roof for sheltering the community as a whole, and smaller places for the groups into which the community occasionally divides itself. In these rooms there must be tables and chairs. In cold weather there must be some heat. If the school is to be a residence school there must be simple residence and dining facilities. Socrates conducted a very successful school without buildings of any kind. The whole school simply stood under a doorway when it rained. The medieval University of Paris, with thousands of students, owned no buildings. The students lived where they could, and the teachers had to provide their own lecture rooms in the city.

Under our present conditions buildings seem to be a necessity, but with our small school they can be small, simple and inexpensive. Ivy climbs just as well on cement block as it does on brick or stone. Fortunately we Americans have no objection to physical work on the part of intellectual people. We must remember that physical work is a definite part of the educational program of our community. Therefore much of the work of maintaining what buildings and grounds there are can be done by teachers and students. It seems absurd to have this work done by a paid staff, and, when the students need exercise, to pay also for the facilities and the staff to provide sports for them. And it is doubly absurd, after having done this absurd thing, to complain that education costs so much.

Our college, if it is to be a residence college, will indeed allow and encourage sports, but they will be on a purely voluntary and spontaneous basis—no compulsion, no paid coaches, a minimum of equipment provided, no bleachers, no charge for any event. Sport will be restored to its proper place: recreation, relaxation in alternation with work.

To achieve wisdom and understanding you must sacrifice many things. Both the process and the goal demand a giving up. To help someone else toward wisdom and understanding you must likewise give up something. Not only students, but teachers and parents also, must make sacrifices if the students are to learn. The man who is learning must make sacrifices as long as he learns, for when sacrifice stops the learning stops too.

I think that here we strive for an ultimate realism, penetrating all the superficial realisms that play such a part in educational propaganda. There is a superficial realism that says in effect, "Get a good education so that you can get a good job. The salary of a man with a college degree is much higher than the salary of one without a degree." And statistics are quoted to prove it. The superficiality is sometimes smeared with a little idealism: "Get a good education so that you will have a good income; and think how much good you can do then!"

But a true realism, a point of view which sees things as they are, would be more like this: If your higher education is successful, so that you come to know, see, and understand actualities, you come to realize that a high income is not important, that the truly valuable possessions and attainments have little to do with dollars, that there really is a connection between plain living and high thinking, and that there is an optimum standard of living whose scale is very modest compared with what is held up as ideal by people who have things to sell. If your education has been successful you will also have developed a sensitivity and concern for people and things which sees that the finest relation to them is not one of possession or mastery, and that therefore the power wealth gives you over people and things is irrelevant and may even be a handicap. Furthermore, it is true that education, like every good thing, is valued in proportion to the sacrifice you make to get it (and give it).

The sacrifice of a standard of living to which many of us have become accustomed may well be the price that a student and a school have to pay for excellence, and when the student and the school make that sacrifice the student is fortunately exempted from paying the dollar price that he would have to pay if he were enduring the commonly accepted standard of living. He need not pay so much for his education in dollars, provided always that he can find a college wise enough to recognize austerity as part of the price of educational excellence.

Ah, but the books! Libraries are expensive. There is no question but that our community of learning would like to have access to all *good* books, and that the reading of good books is a great help in developing one's intellectual powers. But it is also true that the greatest help that reading gives in this education comes when the reading takes place in an atmosphere of thought, meditation and discussion. Theoretically, where an effective dialogue is going on, a person could profit educationally with no books at all, and his memory might be all the keener with no printed word to rely on. But since, other things being equal, good reading enriches everyone, and since the system of education we propose must also provide for the man who shrinks from the dialogue and would prefer to read, we must do our best to supply him with books.

America's conversion to the paper-back book has made it quite possible for a person of limited means to own all the good books really necessary for the kind of higher education that we have been describing. He can own these books, make notes in them, re-read them whenever he wants to, and they can thus be much more a part of him than they could be if they were in a library.

In a school for training expert scholars there is of course need for many expensive and hard-to-get books. But our community of learning has a different purpose and a different plan of education. It will take what good books it can get, of course, but it will never be deterred from exercising its function effectively for the lack of them. The expense of founding and maintaining a fully equipped library will not run up the cost of education in our community.

There are other characteristics of the community which reduce the costs. There will be no complex system of registration for courses, and no keeping track of grades and credits of the students in their progress through our school. Indeed, the only records that will be kept for each student could easily be put on a single card: the date of his admission, the length of his stay, his financial standing with the community, the date of his graduation, and his standing in his class. One person could have charge of these records and spend very little time at it.

With buildings, equipment, maintenance and non-teaching personnel reduced to the minimum, the income of the college could be devoted to the one really important thing: the teachers. But it must be remembered here that the regime of austerity and sacrifice also includes the teachers.

There are teachers in other schools to whom their students come in order to learn how to make more money. Such teachers are presumably interested in making money themselves. If they actually can teach men how to increase their wealth it would not be out of line for them to expect a salary that has some proportion to the financial acceleration that they give to their students.

But our teacher, as a lover of wisdom, looks elsewhere for satisfaction. He is not interested in the money his students will make. He is trying to lead them to wisdom. Part of his work will be to teach them the real value of a dollar: that the dollar is worth while only if it is spent to make someone or some thing better, and that many valuable things are only indirectly—if at all— related to money. In other words, he will try to make them see that the race for money is to a large extent futile and self-defeating. But he cannot possibly make them understand this if he himself is in the race for money. He must of course have enough to support himself and his family on a level which will provide the things that are necessary and really valuable—the same things that he is teaching his students to value. If he seeks more than this his teaching is vitiated by his life. He is not practicing what he is preaching.

Let us be practical. The man who has no idea at all of the joys of the mind and the spirit must have the night club with its artificial excitement to give him a counterfeit happiness. And night clubs are expensive. An evening of conversation can give the wise man a much greater joy, and it doesn't cost anything. A person having interior resources, as presumably the teacher has and hopes his students will have, needs only a minimum of those supposed aids to happiness with which the people in the race for money try to surround their lives.

The doctor of philosophy, therefore, will require only a modest income because of the goal he seeks for himself and his students. He will not demand the salary of a "distinguished" professor. His pay will be within the limits of the power of a small college to grant. He will be willing to make sacrifices to teach in a really effective way. But he will not, and should not, make these sacrifices in order to teach in a way someone else thinks to be effective. The man who is to make a real renunciation for the sake of his teaching must be an autonomous agent, not an employee. This brings us to a discussion of the condition of teachers in the present system of higher education.

The image of the industrial corporation, which has been disastrous when impressed on higher education in the form of courses and credits, has perhaps been equally disastrous in its influence on the persons caught up in the educational system. The management-labor-product syndrome of the manufacturing process is so ingrained that it appears to be the natural way for human enterprise to be carried on. This impresses itself on the educational process in the organizational form of administration-faculty-students, a form protracted over so many decades that few people concerned with education question it. Yet this form, like the course-and-credit pattern, is inimical to the very existence of an educational community.

The students are considered the product, in this way of looking at things. They are things composed of more or less obdurate material, resistant to the shaping hands and tools of the workman. The fact that they have minds makes their obduracy even more intense, and a constant irritation to the workman. The teacher, who is the workman in this analogy, regards the students as an obstacle to be overcome, or even as the enemy. "Pounding knowledge into their heads" is harder than digging ditches. "Getting the best of them" leaves one exhausted and resentful. This attitude of the teacher, which regards the student as a product to be shaped, will not allow a genuinely human relationship to exist between him and the student. There can be no community of learning where it is present.

Why does the teacher develop such an attitude? Because he and everybody else sees his activity in the light of the management-labor-product form. He is *hired* by someone to do a particular job. He is told what to do in the way of teaching, when to do it and when to stop doing it. His success is determined by the

114

approval of those who hired him and, within contractual limits, they can discharge him if he does not please them. In short, he is an employee, and no one should be surprised that he takes on the attitude of an employee, resents whatever the employer does, is dissatisfied with the conditions under which he works, and regards the results of his labor as belonging to someone else and therefore not of vital concern to himself. His desire is to do as little work as possible for as much pay as possible. The students conspire to make this work harder and therefore he resents them too.

Anyone who has attended union meetings and meetings of the faculty with no administrator present will have noticed the great similarity in atmosphere. The union and the faculty in such a situation are the same. Everything the administration does is wrong, and everything that goes wrong is the fault of the administration. Even the manifestly good things the administration does are given a sinister interpretation. I remember that a president once announced that the university was going to give a substantial Christmas present to every faculty child. The comment from the faculty was, "Well, they probably expect us to vote 'company' from now on." This attitude is not a matter of financial desperation. The highest paid members of the faculty share it with those whose salary is lowest. *The attitude does not come from lack of dollars. It comes from lack of dignity.* It comes from the essentially undignified position of the employee, who does not have in his work the autonomy which is the most precious possession of the free man.

Hannah Arendt, in *The Human Condition,* has distinguished between two kinds of human activity, one of which she calls *work* and the other *action.* Work is the activity of making something. It is the activity of the artist, who makes use of material things to carry out an idea that he has in his mind. Subject to the resistance of the material, the artist can realize his idea perfectly. He can be sure that what he intends will be accomplished. He knows that he will deserve, and gain, recognition appropriate to what he has made. Action, however, is something different. It is the activity of a free man in a community of other men who are equally free. Since, once an action is initiated in this community, it becomes subject to the actions of other free men, who also have ideas, and can accept it, resist it, amend it or ignore it, it can never result exactly as its author intended it. No one knows what the result will be. There is an essential precariousness about it all along, and only the historian, after the process has been going on for some time, can tell what happened and can assess the praise or blame to be assigned to what each one has contributed to the whole. Political activity is of this kind. The ancient Greeks regarded it as the most characteristic activity of the free man, an activity where men meet on equal terms and where ability alone determines what happens.

When (and this is no longer Hannah Arendt speaking) the artist uses stone or wood or paint or sound to make something that he has in mind, he is using things that are not morally violated by being so used. One could say that they are meant for this use. But when a man sets out on a work as an artist, and uses *men* as the materials with which he builds, the moral situation is different. Men have ideals, plans and hopes of their own, and there is something essentially inappropriate in using them to carry out ideals and plans that are not theirs. The Greeks would say that such men are not free. We gloss over the moral problem by saying that we are paying free men for their time, and that therefore this time that we pay for—and consequently the activity of the men during this time—is ours and that we can rightfully use it to carry out our plans. But however we justify what we do, the man that we use becomes an employee, and the fact that he almost inevitably takes on an unhealthy attitude toward us and his work may be an indication that there is something morally wrong in our relationship to him. At least it seems to be a relationship that through the ages has bred ill feeling, resentment and rebellion. Apparently men by nature feel uncomfortable when involved in it.

An administrator in a college, as a manager in a factory, is considered successful if he makes something, if he has definite plans and carries them out. He gets all the credit that an artist gets for his creation. But in the process he has done something that the artist has not done. He has used men as means, as instruments, for carrying out his plans. And these men, however highly paid, have been utensils, have lost dignity, have not had opportunity, in the process, of acting as autonomous free men. The good administrator, then, may have been committing an ultimate blasphemy, a blasphemy which cannot be compensated for in reality by the payment of high salaries to those whose human activity he has curtailed.

In our community there will be no such inhuman artistry. The inter-personal activity will be essentially political, not artistic. Every teacher will be a free man who will have a voice in determining what is done. Everyone may initiate action, but what ultimately happens will be the result of the intellectual abrasiveness of the community. The teachers will thus have the dignified position of free men, not employees. The community may not be able to give them very high salaries, but it will give them dignity, which is more valuable. They will be the leading citizens of a free city. And because they are autonomous, and because what the college does is their own doing, the college can ask them without hypocrisy to make financial sacrifices to help along its work. And the sacrifices will be made.

From what we have said it will be clear that this plan for a free city of the mind cannot be imposed on a group of teachers by an administrator. It would be a contradiction of the very idea if a board of trustees were to become interested in the plan and to appoint a president to carry it out in an existing college with a faculty already there. No. The plan will have to be initiated by a group of teachers who already approve of it and are heartily desirous of taking part in it and living under it. The future of the newly created institution will be entirely in their hands. Such teachers will not be hard to find, but they will be quite different from the men turned out by the usual teacher-producing process of our graduate schools.

To return now to what we were discussing at the beginning of this chapter: the efficiency of the small educational institution. Our community of learning, small though it is, will be efficient economically because it does away with absolutely all of the irrelevant accumulation of expensive things, persons and processes that have come to encumber our colleges and universities. It will give a truly basic higher liberal education in the atmosphere of austerity and simplicity which can make possible a great flowering of the mind and the spirit. And because it is congenial to the human mind and spirit it will be efficient educationally. It will make possible the true aim of higher education, in leading young people to the love of wisdom.

* * *

12

There is no denying that our plan for higher education runs counter to contemporary custom. An institution constructed according to this plan would not be like any institution existing anywhere. But this does not mean that it cannot exist. Whenever there is genuine reform, a great part of it consists in the creation of new institutions to embody the new ideals. Indeed, the chief reason for the lack of progress in the contemporary movement of educational reform is that its execution is entrusted to professional educators who naturally wish to maintain the old institutions which they represent.

Our plan is well suited to nourishing the higher intellectual capacities of young people just emerging into adult life. It directs their attention to the important realities and it treats them as men, not as children or as things. The plan is theoretically sound, far more sound than the conventional pattern of education, drawn as it is from the structure and ideals of the industrial corporation, which is actualized in most of our colleges and universities. Our plan is therefore more realistic than this latter plan, even though it is not now a familiar one. Its actualization will require founders and teachers and students who are willing and able to look beyond the walls of convention to a view not shadowed by those walls. They will have to have the spirit of adventure and of daring, the willingness to be disapproved of and perhaps laughed at. They will have to be prepared to risk their reputations and futures for something that has not yet been proved.

Even the process by which this kind of college is established must be different from the usual one. New colleges seem to sprout monthly and there is a conventional way of going about it. A board of trustees is chosen by the founders—usually a political or

119

religious group. This board becomes and remains the ultimate controlling agency of the institution, and the owner of the property connected with it. It proceeds to appoint an administration which then organizes the school and has immediate control over it, deciding its curriculum and appointing its teachers. If an existing institution is to be reformed by the adoption of a new plan of education, the board appoints an administrator to impose the reform on a personnel already there.

It will be evident that this conventional way of establishing or reforming a college cannot be used for implementing our plan of education, for it is entirely at odds with the spirit of the community of learning. A free city cannot be set up this way. There can be no board of trustees outside the community which exercises control in either its establishment or its maintenance, for the community would not then have the necessary autonomy. Nor can there be an administrator appointed by an outside authority to impose the plan on an existing faculty, or even to carry out the plan for a willing faculty.

The teachers in the new school must have control of its inception as well as of its maintenance. No matter what the source of the initial money, the prospective teachers must have the power of decision from the first. They themselves must constitute the ultimate board of control and the legal ownership of the institution. They must be present at the beginning, and their decisions must be the effective force through which the institution comes into being. Any power that they may choose to relinquish must be handed, not back to a board outside the community, but forward to the emerging student body as the whole community begins to take shape.

We have said that the teachers must constitute an already functioning community of learning before any students are received, so that the students as they come will be drawn into a community life that is already there. This means that teachers cannot simply be "hired" to fill the positions that the school will require. The initial step will have to be taken by a group of men, however small, who have the vocation of teaching, who accept the general idea of the plan, and who already know one another and have been accustomed to acting together. These men will constitute the nucleus of the new community, and they can later invite other teachers, admitting them after a period of probation which will test them as members of the community.

I would guess that such teachers will not be hard to find, once the news of the community is proclaimed.

These first teachers will occupy the property of the prospective school and work out the details of its organization, thereby gaining the experience of acting together on the political plane. They will decide when and how the first students will be examined for reception. They will carry out the examinations, receive the accepted students, and start them on their way in the community.

No school can be founded and maintained only by what is paid by the students, except perhaps a school for the very wealthy, which can charge a tuition of considerable proportions. Therefore, since we do not expect such wealthy students, our college must have benefactors. They will be especially needed at the beginning, for there will be a period when the teachers will be working together as a community before any tuition-paying students arrive.

Most men who have wealth enough to enable them to make large gifts to schools have gained their wealth because they have known how to do well within the existing system. They are therefore inclined to respect the system and to have great reverence for the parts of it with which they are not personally familiar. Thus business men who have succeeded in the commercial field are likely to have an awesome regard for educational administrators who have been outstanding in their own pedagogical field (a regard, incidentally, which may be only moderately shared by their fellow educators). It is only natural that these men of wealth should wish to make their presents to schools which are directed by administrators who have already gained prominence, and for educational projects that have the approval of such men.

The same is true of the great philanthropical foundations. Endowed by successful men of the past and administered by the same kind of men, they are very cautious about giving if there is a possibility that their gift might not win approval from men who measure success in tangible increments.

This means that most of the money given for education goes to

121

prominent established institutions for projects that are essentially conventional. The consequence is that the existing pattern of higher education is only strengthened, not reformed. In our attempt to establish a new kind of educational institution there is little hope for help from the traditional benefactors of education.

The benefactors of our school will have to be men of another kind, men who are not simply eager to present themselves as patrons of education, and willing to leave it to the professionals to guide them. If we have patrons they must combine their eagerness with a willingness to assume the responsibility of discovering the nature of higher education and its greatest needs. They must be men willing to risk money on a new thing, a thing obscure up to now, and not likely to afford them much public applause for their giving.

To be consistent with the principles it espouses our school will also require a new way of reaching potential benefactors. Much has been said about the morality of receiving "tainted money." More to the point is the morality of using shady means to persuade potential donors to donate, for this concerns the integrity of the college itself. Much money given to education, quite "pure" in the possession of the donor, becomes tainted by the hands of the school's money-raisers. The drive for funds with its exaggerations, its pressure on the prospective donor, its flattery of men with money, its honorary degrees—this is not at all consonant with moral excellence and ruthless pursuit of truth; and a school that uses such means of raising money cannot seriously maintain the ends it professes to seek, for means influence ends. Therefore, for the school's integrity, it is less important to ask, "Has the man who gives this money come by it honestly?" than to ask, "Have we been perfectly honest with this man in the process by which we got his money?" The request for funds must be made with the same straightforward simplicity, the same love of truth, the same absence of pressure on the human spirit, that we use in the educational process itself. The potential donor must be treated as a free human being who can make up his mind by himself. If he decides not to help us, that decision is as worthy of our respect as his decision to help would be.

Our propaganda must consist only in placing the plan of the

community before people, in answering questions with perfect frankness and, after the community has come into existence, in working to make its results so good that they will speak for themselves. If the means we use in getting started are pure, we can be sure that the results will speak well for the school.

There is one thing to remember: the value of this new plan of higher education lies in its wholeness. Its parts belong together. They will probably not work separately. Therefore the plan cannot be partially implemented. There have been many new experiments in education. Their promoters have been so anxious about getting things going that they have been willing to compromise. The result has been that the new experiment has been so altered in the process of its realization that the new thing has become pretty much like the old, and what you have is a new conventional school, with its unconventionality appearing only in the catalog statements.

There are some very good conventional colleges. There is no need to make more of them simply for the sake of founding something. And the man who wishes to be a real doctor of philosophy will not increase his opportunity of becoming one by going from an old institution to a new one of the same kind.

Therefore, for the sake of higher education and our vocation in it, we who long for the establishment of a true community of learning must restrain our *Baugeist* until it can be employed in building the thing we long for in its entirety.

It will not be a great disaster if our plan cannot be implemented this year. It would be a great disaster if, in order to implement it this year, we were to make so many compromises in the plan that it resulted in something other than a true community of learning.

The plan is good. Our immediate need is to place the matter publicly so that it can be talked about. There are a few people who are now ready and willing to give themselves to it, and their numbers will increase as the plan becomes known. And, when the plan is known, there will be students eager to take part, and men willing to give it the necessary financial support. Then there will be the opportunity to establish a free city of the mind without compromise.

When this will happen depends not upon educational leaders or governments or foundations, but upon people who wish to teach and to learn, and upon people who are willing to help them toward that goal.

* * *

13

When a political body such as the state, or a religious body such as the church, establishes a college or a university, there is always the assumption that the educational institution will be controlled in some measure by the organization that has set it up, both as to the way it is run and as to what will be taught in it. The institution will not be autonomous. It will not be a free city. The teacher will be an employee of some political or religious organization. And therefore the teaching and learning will not be carried on as well as it might be. As we have said before, if teaching and learning are to be at their best, the institution in which these processes are carried on must be free. It must not be administered or controlled by a power outside itself.

But this does not mean that the members of the community may not have a common point of view, a *Weltanschauung,* a source of ultimate inspiration that comes from the outside. When a person wants to teach and believes he has something to give his students, he always has some frame of reference from which he regards the whole, sees what is to be done, and evaluates what he accomplishes. He has made commitments, and always has some commitments to which he hopes to lead his students.

If a group of men were to come together to form a community of learning, even if they were not the spokesmen of any larger organization, they would still have some common point of view, some position from which they looked out at the world. If they lacked this common ground these men would not have come together in the first place.

The men in this founding group would go on to exercise some discretion in choosing others to teach and learn with them, and part of this would consist in seeing that the new teachers and learners shared their viewpoint or were at least sympathetic

125

toward it. They would examine the commitments of the candidates and the knowledge of interest to them, and if these were too different from those of the group the candidates would probably be rejected even though they were otherwise well qualified. The founders would not choose a man, for instance, who, whatever his talents as a teacher might be, was committed to black magic and intended to lead his students to a similar commitment. They would probably not be willing to set up a chair of astrology. They would be unlikely to welcome a man who longed to teach or to learn Chinese medicine. And they would make these refusals not because they had carefully investigated the proposed subjects and found them lacking in truth or value, but because they simply did not accord with their common point of view. They would have the serious intention of treating black magic and acupuncture fairly if these subjects ever came up in discussion, but they would definitely exclude them from the range of commitments desired in the members of the community and the range of subjects to be explicitly investigated there.

They would have to do some such thing if they were to have a community at all. They could not accept everybody. The range of commitments and of interest would have to be criteria for acceptance or rejection. A city of the mind which exists only in the realm of ideas can be thought of as open to any man of any *Weltanschauung* and any commitment, but a community which is actually to exist in this world must have some limits of acceptance and some common ground for its members. And every existing institution of learning, free or not, does have such limits and such a common ground. This is not less true of state universities than of our private church-related colleges. The limits and the common ground are different, but they are there.

In a pluralistic society such as ours there can and should be intellectual societies with many varying points of view. It is only if the point of view is so narrow that it will not allow men to look honestly in any direction that liberal education becomes impossible.

For a great many years liberal education in this country was altogether in the hands of institutions with a Christian commitment. These institutions were not really free cities of the mind, for they were controlled by boards of trustees, but at least it can be said of them that they did their work as well and as broadmindedly as do the secular institutions that have come after them.

The story of the small denominational college is a glorious one in our history. Devoted men came along behind the pioneers, establishing colleges for the education of leaders in the newly rising communities. And devoted people supported them. It is close to the truth to say that from the Appalachians to the Great Plains in our Mid-America at the end of the nineteenth century, a person would rarely be more than fifty miles from one of them. Within a radius of seventy-five miles of my home town in Iowa I can count at least five that survive. Even with the competition of the state universities and land grant colleges they still produce some of the best educated men in the country. I cite these colleges not because they were schools of the kind I propose here, for they were not, but to show that a Christian commitment does not entirely prevent an institution from educating liberally.

I myself am a Catholic Christian, and believe that all things are seen and understood best from a Christian point of view. It is my desire as a teacher in a Catholic university to lead my students to see what I see and understand more than I understand. But there is always frustration, a frustration that does not in the least come from the supposed fact that Catholics are prevented by ecclesiastical authorities from talking about certain things and from following certain lines of investigation. I myself have never experienced such limitation. I have never had an authority say to me, "You mustn't," in anything I wanted to do. But the frustration is there all the same. Some of it is due to the fact that the administration lays down the plan of teaching for teachers and students and leaves little leeway for the unique teacher or student. But the greater part of the frustration is due to the conception of knowledge and its communication current in all American institutions of higher learning, Christian or not.

The scheme of classification of knowledge into separate fields or subjects is as old as Aristotle. For him the sciences were distinct fields of thought, each with its own method and its own first principles, but they were all subsumed under the first and highest science, metaphysics. Thus they were all a part of a hierarchical

127

unity with metaphysics the basic knowledge which gave the original validity to the principles upon which the other sciences were based. The medieval scholastics took this scheme and added theology as the "Queen of Sciences" which gave the illumination of the Christian point of view to the whole structure.

The men of the Enlightenment rejected rather thoroughly the idea of metaphysics as the unifier of sciences, and they completely rejected theology as illuminative knowledge. They were left then with separate sciences ill-connected with one another, but there was hope that the triumphant new experimental-mathematical sciences might supply a method which would purge false knowledge from men's minds and unite the knowledge that remained in one great science. This hope was never completely realized, but the new natural sciences loomed so large in men's thought that all other knowledge was crowded to the periphery of attention. This other knowledge could maintain a trace of dignity only by copying the methods of the natural sciences—detailed research, empirical verification, quantitative measurement.

The new knowledge gave rise to so vast an amount of detail that the scholar hoping to keep abreast of the new discoveries, had to confine himself to one small area of knowledge. And if the scholar happened to be a teacher he was supposed to confine his teaching to the one small area in which he had specialized. Any departure by the teacher from the "subject" he was supposed to be teaching was regarded as a sign of incompetence.

The "subject," or field of specialty, came to be regarded as an entity which had an existence of its own which could command the teacher. It could determine what he could say and could not say. It was, you might say, a distinct package of knowledge, separated from the other packages, and remaining intact no matter who taught it or who studied it. Its relations with other subjects, if they were considered at all, were thought to be part of another package labelled "philosophy," a subject which had to be taught separately.

Our Christian educators have accepted this ideal of knowledge, secular though its foundations may have been, and have tried to introduce religion and theology into this strictly secular system as merely an additional package. They have assumed with the others that physics is physics—a self-contained reality excluding all that is not itself—and that biology is biology and history, history. And their students have carried this thought process a little farther: theology is just theology, a distinct and separate package of knowledge (and a rather second class one at that, because state universities do not teach it).

In such a situation the Christian teachers have found it very difficult to lead their students to look at a thing—at all things—from a really Christian point of view, and because they have found difficulty here they have found difficulty in leading their students to that attitude of joy and worship which should characterize those who seek God.

They try to play the educational game according to rules laid down by people who have rejected or ignored the Christian faith, and they wonder why it has been so hard to bring faith into the game. They consequently go about with an air of bewilderment, almost pleading with their students and with the world to give at least a little attention to religion.

As we said when discussing the theological way of knowing, when a person is a convinced Christian everything looks different from the way it looks to a secularist. Therefore a Christian cannot teach a "subject" or a person in the same way that a secularist would teach that same subject and that same person. Teaching is not just a matter of transferring the content of a package of knowledge to the mind of the student. It is a matter of one person trying to show another person all that he sees in a certain area of reality. And one person may see much that another cannot see. If he sees it he is frustrated when the rules of the profession, set up by people who do not see certain things, require that these things not be mentioned.

Physics is not simply physics or history, history. All these sciences have different overtones, as they are taught and learned by different people. Their degree of certainty is different. Teachers and students do not always make the same inferences from them. For some minds there is a beauty in them, for some only utility. For some there is a finality about them and they can become the final court of appeal; for others the sciences themselves need the support of a kind of faith. The secular teacher does not teach without giving overtones, without expressing preferences, although he may think that he does. He gives a set of preferences that might be said to be official, the preferences that tend to make of science the supreme knowledge and the criterion of all other knowledge, and the scientific method the only reliable method for coming to know anything. The Christian cannot see things this way.

We have found many reasons for departing from the conventional plan of American higher education. We now find for the Christian an additional and most important reason: the conventional plan is slanted in the direction of a disregard of God. As a Catholic I would insist that the prevailing plan of Catholic higher education, which follows the conventional American plan quite slavishly, hinders its own specifically Catholic and Christian aims. Indeed, I would expect that this proposal for a free city of the mind would meet with as much opposition from conventional Catholic educators as from American educators in general.

The plan of the free city was not designed explicitly for the Christian teacher but for the human teacher—as a means to liberate all the human powers for the teaching-learning process. We tend to cramp our own enterprises with an accumulation of irrelevant customs, conventions and the relics of past effectiveness, so that every enterprise needs liberation if it continues for any length of time. But the free city liberates the Christian teacher along with other teachers. For one thing, the teacher, according to this plan, is not restricted to his special subject. He must have a part in the whole learning process of the student. He is supposed to communicate all the shades, colors and overtones that he himself sees and hears. Higher education is approached by way of the great realities to be known and the different ways of knowing them rather than by way of the different sciences or fields of knowledge presented separately. Finally, the emphasis on understanding would lead the student to see the necessity of focusing *all* his knowledge on the reality being studied, and when this reality is God the knowledge will be much more than theology.

The free city of the mind, then, would make it possible for the full power and beauty of Christianity to function freely in liberal higher education. The cost of such a small institution is within

130

the capability of Christian men who wish to do something for Christian education and do not have tax money at their disposal. The present reaction against the gigantism of our great universities ought to make people more aware of the value of small schools and personal contact between teacher and learner.

We ought to see many of these small colleges established under the auspices (not the control) of Christian bodies, colleges which could become the intellectual centers of their regions in a way that complex universities could never be.

The disunity of Christianity has been scandal for a long time, and has gone a long way toward obscuring its power and beauty. But in these last years the ecumenical movement has begun—just begun—to reveal the possibility that the damage may be sometime repaired. There is a new wind of understanding and cooperation blowing. This brings about an educational opening that was unthinkable a few years ago. It now seems possible that teachers and learners who are convinced Christians might work together as free associates in an institution of higher learning which is controlled neither by the state nor by any religious denomination. Our free city of the mind would supply a satisfactory form for such an institution, which could be a most effective agent for expressing and strengthening a Christianity beginning to feel itself one.

Christianity, however, is a very broad term, and the common ground of all those "who profess and call themselves Christians" would perhaps be meager. But there are groups of Christians who have enough in common to allow a community to be established.

The founding group of the community I propose (and I do not here rule out the advisability of the establishment of similar communities organized by non-Christians) would be made up of people from different religious bodies who sincerely accept what is perhaps the earliest Christian creed: *Jesus is Lord,* not just a great teacher or an inspiring personality but the Lord, the Master, to whom allegiance is owed. These people would also agree in having a sense of the historic dimension of Christianity and an appreciation of the liturgical worship of God. Such men would most likely be Orthodox, Anglican, Lutheran or Roman Catholic; but individuals from other religious bodies or from none might qualify by having such personal beliefs.

But this agreement in conviction is not enough. The members of the initial community must be able to get along together. They must be the kind of people who are willing and able to work in close association with others whose opinions on many things may be different from their own, without trying to defeat them in argument or win them over to their own position. Yet they must all have strong religious convictions. Indifference toward things Christian is not a good foundation on which to build an inter-Christian educational community which will actualize strong and effective faith. What we are saying is that these first members of the new city of the mind must have both strong convictions and a deep love.

When originally describing the community of learning we said that it would be well if the original group consisted of people who were already working together. This would be doubly necessary if the group were to be made up of sincerely convinced Christians from different denominations, for in recent tradition it has been just these sincerely convinced men, as distinct from those who are indifferent, who have been the carriers of interdenominational antagonisms. If there is to be an ecumenical free city with an actively Christian basis its first members must *know* that they can work together in spite of the tensions inherent in their traditions; and they can only know this if they actually *have* worked together.

There is yet another difficulty. If the venture is to succeed it can only do so if the authorities of the various denominations to which its members belong do not oppose it. To go against existing authorities in the name of ecumenism would be in effect to set up another sect, and thus to violate the very spirit of ecumenism. Therefore our ecumenical free city could not be set up just anywhere. It would have to be brought into being in a place where all local authorities concerned were interested and willing to have it happen, without having any desire to control it.

Granted that the nucleus-community of teachers is established with the good will of the religious bodies from which the teachers come, what then? These men will begin to function as a community by engaging in a dialogue. They will, in this discussion, draw up a plan of studies for themselves and for their prospective students; and they will receive these students to the number decided on and with the testing that they have adopted. Remember that once the community is started it will be autonomous. This means that we can no longer legislate for it. We can only suggest and speculate.

The first students would probably be drawn mostly from the religious bodies from which the teachers have come. They would come because they had heard of the plan and its actualization and because they wished for a Christian education at its fullest. In every new movement a large lunatic fringe gathers, and so among the first applicants to the new college there would probably be an abnormally large proportion of essentially unstable people. Since the initial success of the community depends on the stability and character of the first students as well as on the quality of the first teachers, extra care would have to be taken at first to exclude those students who might make a community of learning impossible.

There is another point to be brought up. The community is established to give liberal education from a Christian point of view, and yet it does not include teachers from all the Christian bodies. How can the teaching help but be biased? And if the community includes only Christian teachers how can other points of view be fairly presented? No school, however broad-minded, could employ a committed teacher for every known intellectual or religious position, and views can only be explained fairly by men who honestly believe in them. This is a universal problem for people who want to be just and fair to all. Its solution can never be entirely satisfactory.

To bring into the teaching body representatives of every set of convictions would be as impossible for our free city as for any institution. Since it is autonomous, however, its membership can at any time choose to bring into its fellowship a teacher with a new point of view if such a thing seems desirable. It will be more elastic in this way than other schools. Besides this, and perhaps more importantly, the plan gives a real place in the teaching-learning process to visitors who come to stay for a period of time. They can present their case in the formal dialogue and then spend time in informal discussion with students who wish to talk with them.

Such visitors would not be permanent members of the community and therefore would not have to fit into it, either by conviction or by temperament. At the same time, while at the school they would have free opportunity to present their case as well as they could. There would be no censoring of what they might say, no interfering with their private meetings with either teachers or students. It is hard to image a fairer method of presenting points of view not found among the permanent teachers of the community.

There is one task that must be begun for the benefit of the whole of Christianity. This is the task of working out a scheme of Christian education for people of what we call college age. At the most, what we have now is secular education with some Christian trimmings.

The ancient Greeks developed a complete scheme of education designed to give the younger generation the good things of the past and at the same time train their mind and bodies to the height of perfection. That scheme, which they called the *Paideia* was in general taken over by the Roman world and served as the means of education for the whole classical age. St. Augustine received this education, and when he became a Christian he began to devote his life to working out a way of educating Christian young men which would give them all the values of Christianity and all that was worth while in the classical learning. It was to be a Christian *Paideia*. The medieval scholastics also had a *Paideia*, based on a reconciliation of Aristotelian thought and science (the latest thing at the time, which dazzled the world by its completeness) with Christian Theology.

We have a real need now of a new Christian *Paideia*, for none of the old ones can deal satisfactorily with the new knowledge, the new thought-values and the new points of view. We need a genuinely Christian recognition of all that is new and valuable, without ignoring anything that is old and valuable. We need minds that are able to look at all thought without flinching, minds that are able to see everything in the light of providence and salvation.

It may well be that our ecumenical free city will be the place where such a modern Christian *Paideia* can be worked out. There will be a freedom there to cross the barriers between fields of thought. There will be a dialogue there that will bring all the members and all possible subjects of discussion into the arena. There will be criticism at every step of the thinking, criticism both positive and negative. And there will be people "living with the subject" constantly. There will also be a freedom of time for there will be few administrative duties, and the ordinary chores of the classroom will be lightened.

A great university, even a Christian one, might hesitate to undertake this task of working out a *Paideia* except as a job for the Department of Education. If the university as a whole should focus its attention on it it would lose prestige. (What would Harvard think?) Our free city, at least in the beginning, would be in the blessed situation of not having any prestige to lose. The Free City of the Mind could be of great service to the City of God. It could serve its Master and His brothers freely in doing what most needs to be done.

I must add this post-script for those who, knowing my personal commitment to the Christian interpretation of history, may misunderstand my argument and assume that the colleges I should like to see brought into existence would necessarily be Christian colleges. I have sketched my preference only as an example but I do not thereby rule out the establishment of similarly organized colleges with a constellation of teachers having a different central interest and philosophical direction. I do not mean to say that the criterion of Christianity should be a requirement for the kind of college I propose but only that, among all the possible perspectives, this is the one in which I myself am particularly interested. The establishment of such an ecumenically oriented community does not preclude the establishing of another on a different basis. But it seems to me that until such communities of learning have been founded our educational system will continue to offer its customers the attractively pre-packaged culture which streams down the assembly line of the ivy-covered factory.

AFTERWORD

It is only fair, both to the reader and to myself, to present evidence that this proposal for a new pattern of higher liberal education does not spring from a mere desire to be different or a petulant dissatisfaction with my own position and prospects in the academic world, which in fact I think to be the most completely satisfying available to me or anyone else within the existing academic structure. But, happy as I am in it, I am firmly convinced that the educational pattern within which teachers in liberal arts colleges work is thoroughly and intrinsically wrong, so that the men who most sincerely strive for the full intellectual development of their students must suffer almost continual frustration, and can accomplish their work only to the extent that they refuse to conform to the pattern.

As a faculty child brought up on the fringes of the State University of Iowa, I was associated from the beginning with scholars and administrators. As a result of this familiarity, and with the low level of my childish vision, I saw the feet of clay of these people before I looked up to appreciate the nobility that was sometimes also there. I saw that they were often opinionated, factional, and only by a stretch of the imagination wise. The words "president," "dean," "professor" and "scholar" roused no awe or respect in me. These men were a dime a dozen, and I knew what my father thought of most of them. Later, when I became a student at the University, I found to my surprise that some of them were really great teachers. Prof. G. T. W. Patrick, Prof. Charles B. Wilson, Prof. Charles Heald Weller, Prof. Clarence M. Case, Prof. Gilbert G. Benjamin, and my own father, C. C. Nutting, are the ones that stand out in my memory.

But none of these men to whom I was attracted and by whom I was helped seemed to have any interest in me as a person to be liberally educated. Not one of them made an effort to discern or to remedy the defects in my education which were becoming apparent even to me. As long as I was interested in what *they* were interested in they liked me, but none of them took any thought beyond his field of interest. An exception was my own father, who of course had a special responsibility for me and who, though a zoologist, persuaded me to study Greek. But that is as far as anyone's non-specialism went. The result was that mathematics and the whole field of art and literature were empty for me, and became emptier as time went on, for none of the teachers in those fields, although some were supposed to be good, touched me at all. It was another thirty years before I had any idea of what creative writing was about. No one, apparently, was concerned with the whole of my education.

That I was dissatisfied is shown by a protest I almost made in my junior year. I was to speak on behalf of the students who were being received into Phi Beta Kappa. I prepared a talk that was supposed to be blistering, to the effect that no one on the faculty, not even the Phi Beta Kappas, seemed to have any regard for the fraternity's motto: *Philosophy the Pilot of Life;* that they were wrapped up in studies which they did not try to integrate with their own lives or the lives of their students; and that our high school teachers had done a much better job in this very important aspect of education. When the time came to deliver this tirade I gave a very halting and very conventional speech of gratitude for the honor done to us. I still cringe at my hypocrisy and cowardice.

During my undergraduate days my most time-consuming study —the study that absorbed more of my interest than all of the rest together—was the investigation of what was for me a newly discovered thing: Christianity. This study was carried on under the initial inspiration of the Rev. Paul Boynton James, Rector of the Episcopal Church in Iowa City. It was entirely extra-curricular, of course, since none of the courses I was taking had anything to do with it. It was almost illicit; it could not be taught in courses without raising the question of church and state. My teachers, parents, and friends considered it a waste of time. And yet this was by far the most valuable educational experience of my life. It established a point of view which I have never found inadequate, a pattern in which one is encouraged to develop morally, intellectually, and spiritually in all possible directions and within which there are no barriers to inquiry. And this most valuable education I could get only by ignoring the advice of all the official teachers of the university. In this situation I came to appreciate the value of unofficial teachers.

Mr. James was such a one. He had the great ability to inspire a person to go farther than he himself had gone, and the humility to rejoice when he was excelled by his pupils. I found rather soon that his knowledge of, say, church history was not too profound, but he was always encouraging me to make mine more profound. And so it was throughout the area of Christian studies. He was taking some work at the university, so that we were in a way fellow students. And always, whether we were studying together or I was studying independently, he was encouraging me to go deeper. Through him, whom I consider one of my best teachers, I learned that one does not have to be an authority or an expert in a field of study to be a most successful teacher there.

Having had this so completely profitable experience of studying on my own, with the help of a friend and of books, I could of course no longer consider the course and credit system of education to be supremely important. I had definitely learned more outside the established pattern than within it.

After graduating from Iowa with a much better education than the authorities and teachers of the university intended to give me, and having obtained it by not following the plan which the University curriculum outlined for me, I had the wonderful experience of three years at Oxford, where I continued my Christian studies. Here I had my first realization of what an educational institution could be. I worked under a really great teacher, the late Canon D. C. Simpson, then a tutor at Keble College and later the Oriel Professor of Scriptural Interpretation. Mr. Simpson was what might be called a total teacher. He was interested in his students as men. He lectured to us, he tutored us, he urged us, shamed us, showed up our laziness and our ignorance, and above all, loved us. He would call us together at unexpected times (in his rooms at midnight, for instance) when he wanted to be sure that we understood a point. When he was ill we met at his bedside. When my eyes failed so that for almost a year I could not read, he provided a reader for me, and Mrs. Simpson set aside a room in their house where the reader and I could meet in the evenings. Mr. Simpson was firm, almost ruthless, in his treatment of us. In our American school system I had always been handled with gloves, and it was some time before I realized that his apparent hardness concealed a genuine and deep love, and was only used to spur us on.

The men who were or had been his pupils thought of themselves as a kind of privileged fraternity. There were four of us in the inner circle of that fraternity—Charles L. Taylor, Harold M. Sanders, John Stewart MacArthur, and myself. It was a blessed little community and has remained so, for after forty years we still think of ourselves as such. Mr. Simpson and Harold Sanders have left us, but Mrs. Simpson still lives in Oxford and is the focal point for us. This association showed me what a community of learning could be, where there is true comradeship and where everyone learns from everyone else. I am particularly grateful to Stewart MacArthur, an older man than the other three of us, who by word and life taught me the sanctity of the human person, a sanctity not to be violated by pressure or by pleading.

But the community of learning at Oxford was for me much wider than this blessed circle. All around us were young men interested in things of the mind. Everywhere there was discussion, disputation and cooperative study of all conceivable subjects. Wherever two or three met, the discussion got going. Intellectual interest was self-propelling. It did not require a teacher to push it into being or to keep it in operation. It was outside the formal periods of instruction that a very great part of our teaching and learning went on, and no subject was left untouched for very long.

It was also at Oxford, where I saw a great university almost completely without an administration, that I came to realize the great harm the administrative element does in higher education by imposing a pattern—chiefly to fit administrative considerations—within which teachers and learners *must* carry on the process of education, and by claiming for itself the right of final decision.

Back at Iowa for graduate work after six years out in the world, I met another great teacher, Prof. Herbert Feigl. He had recently come from Europe and had not in the least been influenced by the American academic pattern, which he proceeded to disregard in every way. He was interested, it appeared, in only one thing: that we should understand. The whole standard procedure was forgotten. He did not remember to make assignments. There was no written work. He forgot about examinations. He thought only of his subject and us. He was wonderfully clear in his exposition. He could make a person see what he meant, and the importance of it. In spite of the fact that there was no compulsion in his courses and no day of reckoning at the end of them, I neglected everything else and concentrated my attention on what he was teaching. Almost every waking hour for two solid years was devoted to thinking about his ideas, and to reviewing everything I knew and believed in the light of them. I suppose this is what is meant by a challenge.

I was by no means Prof. Feigl's disciple. I disagreed with almost everything that he stood for, but his exposition of his fundamental positions was so clear and so forceful that I had to examine my own position very keenly in order to be able to maintain it. It was, as a matter of fact, during my association with this brilliant logical positivist that I was able to give intellectual consolidation to my status as a newly arrived Catholic.

When I came back to Iowa the country was in the midst of the great depression. I wished to study modern philosophy because I wanted to understand it. I also needed a scholarship in order to be able to do this. Dean Carl E. Seashore, a friend of the family, advised against modern philosophy for practical reasons. He said that if I took a doctorate in this field I could never get a job teaching it in a state school because I was a Catholic, and I could never get a job teaching it in a Catholic school because I had studied it in a state school. I had to decide right then a question most important for education: do you study in order to get a job or in order to understand? I decided that understanding was more intrinsic to a person than a job was; and with as gentle a stubbornness as I could manage I insisted that, job or no job, I wanted to study modern philosophy. The Dean was kind enough to give me a scholarship for it. Incidentally, he was right. I never have had the job of teaching philosophy.

Here in the graduate school I came face to face with a rather horrifying situation. I found estimable young men working very hard, and being urged and driven on by their teachers, to come to know more and more about less and less. It was not the close investigation of their subject that was horrifying; it was their disinclination and even their inability to think and talk about anything else. And the specialization extended within the fields of study. In one history seminar that I attended, the students of the French Revolution seemed to regard it as an insult to their dedication to be asked a question about Louis XI. These men were being ruined as prospective guides for young people in their intellectual development. They would get the degree of doctor of philosophy if they worked hard enough, but by this very work for this very degree they were being prevented from becoming what the title *Doctor of Philosophy* means: Teacher of the Love of Wisdom.

After I had been teaching for eighteen years according to the conventional academic pattern, and undergoing constant frustration because I was becoming ever more aware that the important goal in the education of men was wisdom rather than a knowledge of history, there came a great release. Father John Cavanaugh, then president of Notre Dame, established a new "department" which came to be called the General Program of Liberal Studies, a way of teaching and learning somewhat after the model of the plan of St. John's College, Annapolis.

In establishing the General Program, Father Cavanaugh acted with a wisdom seldom shown by administrators. He did not impose the plan on anyone. The new faculty was composed of men who earnestly wanted to make the experiment. And once the thing was set up, he did not try to run it, but allowed the faculty as complete an autonomy as the most general regulations and policies of the university would permit. These regulations and policies do indeed prevent the program from becoming as real a community of learning as one could hope for, but compared to what goes on generally in the country the grass is green, and it is a privilege to work with the faculty and students who constitute a much more real community than can be found elsewhere.

During the academic year 1956-57 I had the opportunity to take part in an educational experiment in the microscopic University of Melbourne, Florida. Here was a glorious year-long experience of sending academic proprieties to the devil—departments, fields of knowledge, scholastic reputations and such —and getting down to an earnest effort to bring all available knowledge and as much wisdom as we could muster to bear on certain very important problems of living. There were not many people concerned, all of them adults and none of them bound by the conventional American ideas of higher education.

The institution was held together by a small but heroic group of people among whom were Virginia Wood, Mary Frances Peirce, and my sister, Elizabeth Nutting. The presiding officer at the time was Ralph Borsodi, who had also conceived the school plan. In him I met a man who was raised outside the academic tradition, and who focused his keen intellect on all problems from a new point of view. It seemed to me that, while he had missed a lot by being outside this tradition, he had valuable insights into many things which came from figuring things out for himself, and which would never have come to him had he been academically trained.

Don Gospill was, so far as the records went, a student there, and I was a teacher, but in that free fellowship the distinction fell away, and he, a man of great wisdom, took the place which his excellence deserved, and for much of the time he was the teacher of us all.

Into this little community there came for a very short time the late Dr. Hermann Reichenbach, a musician-physicist and pupil of Einstein. I think that most of us regard his stay with us as the high point in the teaching-learning experience of the year. A person could never be the same after undergoing an educational year like this one.

Since that time I have been conducting, under the sponsorship of my university, a small class of adults where we do just what we want to. We are now in our seventh year of existence and have developed something of a community. There is no place where the distinction between teacher and learner means less, and there is no situation from which I have learned more. We know each other very well now. At the beginning of each year we decide what we are going to do. The first two years we discussed the problems proposed at Melbourne. Then we took up some problems of our own. Then we studied some books. In this atmosphere of freedom we all learn. I wish to express my gratitude especially to two men who have been in this group from the beginning: Adam Meyers and Otis Romine.

In this life-long experience, almost all of it concerned with education, I have come to the definite conclusion that the forms under which higher education takes place in this country—the form under which students and teachers associate and the form by which teachers and administrators are related—are a positive hindrance to intellectual development.

As a Catholic Christian, to whom Christianity is the most valuable enlightenment, I have come to some other conclusions. It is not only the form of higher education in this country that is defective. It is the content also. Knowledge has been divided into "fields" which must be taught each by its own expert who must remain strictly within that field. You add all the fields together and you have the whole of knowledge. Back in Iowa City there was a discussion group of university people and other "intellectuals." One most unlikely member was an old Lutheran minister who was not an intellectual at all, but not therefore unwise. He would doze through the discussions, arousing himself at infrequent intervals only to ask in a rather discouraged voice, "Where does God come in in all this?" He was right. Where does He? Knowledge has been so organized as to leave God out. He is not denied; but, every field of knowledge being adequate in itself for itself, there is simply no need of Him anywhere. Such a situation balks a Christian teacher at every turn. No matter which of the conventional subjects he teaches, he finds it impossible to use that Christian knowledge which is to him the most valuable of all.

Our Catholic colleges have tried to handle the situation by bringing into the curriculum another subject: theology. But, and here is another conclusion of which I am convinced, theology introduced this way comes to be regarded by the students as a

143

kind of superadded thing, somewhat out of place and not to be taken as seriously as, say, physics or history. And everyone agrees that theological knowledge and the Christian point of view should not be intruded into courses of physics or history.

All this is paralyzing to the Christian teacher. This organization of knowledge frustrates him. If a student is to be led to understand the Christian perspective from which all things are to be seen, the Christian teacher must not be bound by the conventional compartmentalizing of knowledge. He must approach the totality of things from a new direction if he is to do his very best for his students. I have tried to suggest here what this new direction might be.

Having thus come to the conviction that our American scheme of liberal education does not do what it might do for some very wonderful young people, I have dared to propose another plan, in which both form and content are departures from the prevailing pattern.

I wish to thank Roland Ramirez, once a student at Notre Dame and now at Duquesne University, for starting me to think seriously about a new form of higher liberal education. He wrote an essay in which he raised a serious problem. The human mind being made for knowing, he said, should find coming to know a very joyful process. Instead, it is most often a toilsome chore. Something must be wrong with the way we teach people to know. I set about trying to figure out a plan of teaching and learning in which coming to know would have the joy that it is meant to have.

Three men have been closely associated with me from the time this plan began to take shape. Father Thomas Brennan (whom we call "Junior" to distinguish him from another priest with the same name), a very remarkable teacher, first showed me the value of metaphysical knowing among the ways of knowing. Julian Pleasants and Paul Delker, younger men, possess to a remarkable degree that Christian wisdom and understanding at which liberal education aims. I am grateful for all the help these three have given me and it would be my great joy if we could all be together as teachers in a free city of the mind.

* * *